ENLIVEN
ENCOUNTERING GOD
Through
HIS WORD

DANIEL

A PATH TO FAITHFUL WITNESS

All Scripture quotations, unless otherwise indicated, are taken from the New American Standard Bible® (NASB), Copyright © 1960, 1962, 1963, 1968, 1971, 1972, 1973, 1975, 1977, 1995 by The Lockman Foundation Used by permission. www.Lockman.org

Scripture quotations marked AKJV are taken from the *Authorized King James Version*. KJV reproduced by permission of Cambridge University Press, the Crown's patentee in the UK.

Scripture quotations marked NKJV are taken from the *New King James Version®*. Copyright © 1982 by Thomas Nelson. Used by permission. All rights reserved.

Scripture quotations marked KJV are taken from the
King James Version of the Holy Bible.

Scripture quotations marked ESV are taken from the Holy Bible, *English Standard Version*, copyright © 2005. Used by permission of the Standard Bible Society. Used by permission.

ISBN: 978-1-940682-66-2

ALL RIGHTS RESERVED. No portion of this publication may be reproduced, stored in a retrieval system, or transmitted in any form or by any means—electronic, mechanical, photocopy, recording, or any other—except for brief quotations in printed reviews, without the prior permission of Church of God Adult Discipleship.

Copyright © 2019 by Church of God Adult Discipleship, Cleveland, Tennessee

Printed in the United States of America

ILLUSTRATIONS

Map of the Ancient Near East in the Time of Daniel
    (attribution: Lee Roy Martin)

The Fiery Furnace—A Painting in the Catacombs
    (Attribution: Public Domain)

The Fiery Furnace—Heures d'Henri II (1429)
    (Attribution: G. Garitan, https://creativecommons.org/licenses/by-sa/4.0/deed.en. Image was altered.)

Nebuchadnezzar Dreams of a Great Tree (Ars moriendi, Marseille—BM—ms. 0089)
    (Attribution: Public Domain)

Nebuchadnezzar Regains His Sanity—by Jacob Symonsz Pynas
    (Attribution: Public Domain)

Belshazzar Sees the Handwriting on the Wall—by Rembrandt
    (Attribution: Public Domain, Purchased by the National Gallery with support of The Art Fund)

Daniel in the Den of Lions—by Daniel Briton Riviere (1840–1920)
    (Attribution: Manchester Art Gallery, Public Domain)

Bust of Alexander the Great
    (Attribution: British Museum, Photograph © Andrew Dunn, Dec. 3, 2004, http://creativecommons.org/licenses/by-sa/2.0/deed.en. Image was not altered.)

Coin with Likeness of Antiochus IV Epiphanes
    (Attribution: Classical Numismatic Group, Inc. http://www.cngcoins.com, https://creativecommons.org/licenses/by-sa/3.0/deed.en. Image was not altered.)

Daniel Touched by Gabriel
    (Attribution: Paid Commercial License, ClipArt ETC)

Daniel Before King Cyrus—by Rembrandt
    (Attribution: Public Domain)

Table of Contents

A Brief Background to the Book of Daniel vii

Introduction to an Inductive Study of Daniel xiii

Lesson 1 Faithful Witness in Challenging Times (Daniel 1:1-21) 1

Lesson 2 Faithful Witness Through the Holy Spirit (Daniel 2:1-49) 19

Lesson 3 Faithful Witness Unto Death (Daniel 3:1-30) 43

Lesson 4 Faithful Witness of God's Sovereignty (Daniel 4:1-37) 63

Lesson 5 Faithful Witness of God's Judgment (Daniel 5:1-31) 87

Lesson 6 Faithful Witness of God's Deliverance (Daniel 6:1-28) 111

Lesson 7 Faithful Witness of God's Kingdom (Daniel 7:1-28) 133

Lesson 8 Faithful Witness of the Last Days (Daniel 8:1-27) 157

Lesson 9 Faithful Witness through Prayer and Fasting (Daniel 9:1-27) 181

Lesson 10 Faithful Witness in Light of the End (Daniel 10:1–12:13) 207

Concluding Remarks 241

About the Author 243

Our Father who art in heaven,
Hallowed be Thy name.
Thy kingdom come. Thy will be done,
On earth as it is in heaven.
Give us this day our daily bread.
And forgive us our debts,
as we also have forgiven our debtors.
And do not lead us into temptation,
but deliver us from evil.
For Thine is the kingdom,
and the power,
and the glory,
forever.
Amen
(Matthew 6:9-13 NASB 1977).

The Brief Background to the Book of Daniel

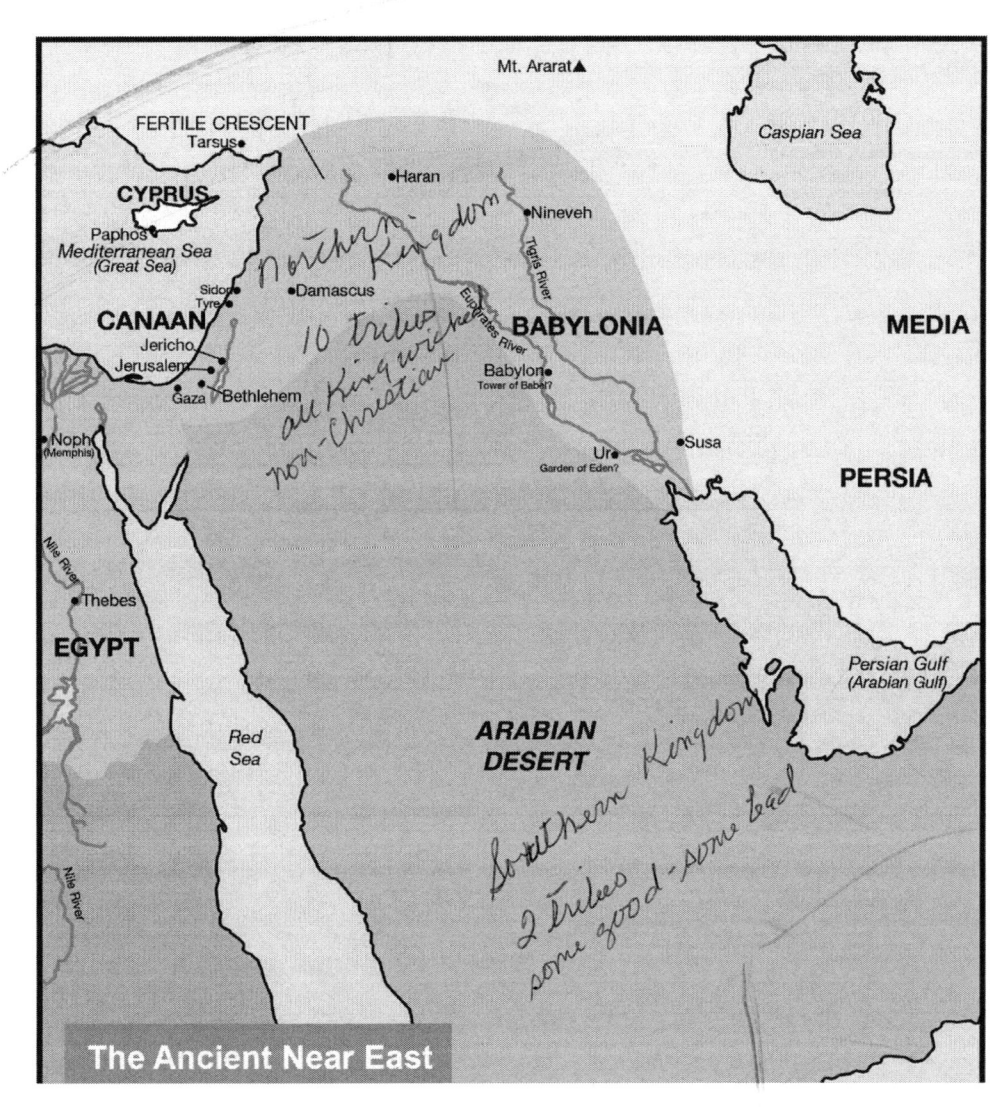

The Content of the Book of Daniel

Whenever someone mentions the Book of Daniel, we immediately think of the story of Daniel in the lions' den, or we might remember the miraculous deliverance of the three Hebrews from the fiery furnace. These miracle stories have been told to children throughout history, and they have been popular subjects for preaching and for inclusion in Bible story books. However, the mention of Daniel may also remind us of the deep mysteries regarding the last days and the end of the world—what scholars call *eschatology* (which means the "study of last things").

There is a good reason why we think of two very different subjects—miracle stories and mysteries of the end—when we reflect on the Book of Daniel. We think of Daniel in these two ways because of the format of the book itself. The Book of Daniel consists of twelve chapters. The first six chapters narrate a series of stories about Daniel and his friends who are in exile in Babylon. Then, the last six chapters relate Daniel's dreams and visions regarding the future destiny of the Jewish people. The miracle stories demonstrate clearly that God is able to care for His people even when they are in very difficult and challenging situations. The mysteries regarding the end show us that God is in control of world history;

therefore, we should not worry about the future or be paralyzed with fear. As God's people, we can maintain a *faithful witness* to the world of unbelievers if we will trust in God's goodness and if we will live in the knowledge that the end is near. In His care for us and in His governance of the world, God is sovereign.

The Historical Context of Daniel

In the English Bible, Daniel is the fourth of the major prophets, following Isaiah, Jeremiah, and Ezekiel. The prophets Isaiah and Jeremiah rebuked the Israelites for their sins (particularly their idolatry and their abuse of the weakest members of the community), and they predicted that God would judge these sins. They foresaw the rise of the Babylonian Empire and that empire's domination of the ancient Near East. They prophesied that God would punish Israel by allowing the Babylonians to conquer Israel and take them into captivity. Near the end of his life, the prophet Jeremiah saw his predictions come to pass. King Nebuchadnezzar of Babylon laid siege to Jerusalem and eventually destroyed both the city and its holy Temple. As young men, the prophets Ezekiel and Daniel were taken captive and carried off to Babylon, where they lived in exile for the rest of their lives. The Book of Daniel tells the story of Daniel's life in Babylonian captivity.

Daniel as Apocalyptic Literature

It was mentioned previously that the Book of Daniel, especially chapters 7–12, are eschatological, that is, concerning the last things. Furthermore, Daniel is a particular type of eschatological literature that is called *apocalyptic*. The word *apocalyptic* means an "unveiling" or an "uncovering" of secret mysteries. The Book of Revelation is also included in the category of apocalyptic literature. Apocalyptic literature is different from other types of prophecy in that it includes visions of heaven, visits by angels, representations of symbolic creatures, the figurative use of numbers, and predictions of God's sudden and powerful intervention to bring about His kingdom on earth. Apocalyptic prophecies like those of Daniel speak to us when our faith has been challenged and when the normal structures of the community are either threatened or have collapsed. Therefore, apocalyptic represents a crisis literature; and it is intended to offer comfort and hope to the afflicted. Furthermore, apocalyptic writings point to spiritual realities that are unseen by the natural eye. Heaven may be unseen, but it is real; and all earthly powers, though inflicting much pain, will soon be reduced to insignificance in the ultimate sense. God has promised to intervene in history and to impose His rule upon the earth. Apocalyptic literature such as Daniel was relevant for the ancient audience, and it is relevant for us today. This kind of writing speaks a powerful word to three different audiences. First, to the oppressed, deprived, and alienated, apocalyptic literature describes God's alternative order, which will free them from the one under which they now suffer. Second, it speaks a warning to the oppressors, whether they are conscious or not of obstructing God's order of compassion and justice. Third, to the wavering—the ones who cannot decide whether to trust fully in God or to trust in human ideologies and military-political strategy—this genre serves as a "wake-up!" call.

An Outline of the Book of Daniel

The following outline represents the basic structure of the Book of Daniel.

I. Faithful Witness in Challenging Times (1:1-21)

    A. Daniel's Captivity (1:1-7)

    B. Daniel's Steadfastness (1:8-16)

    C. Daniel's Miraculous Wisdom (1:17-21)

II. Faithful Witness Through the Holy Spirit (2:1-49)

    A. Nebuchadnezzar Dreams About a Statue (2:1-6)

    B. God Reveals the Dream to Daniel (2:7-23)

    C. Daniel Gives the Interpretation to Nebuchadnezzar (2:24-45)

    D. Daniel Is Promoted (2:46-49)

III. Faithful Witness Unto Death (3:1--0)

    A. Confronted With Idolatry (3:1-12)

    B. Refusal to Bow Down (3:13-18)

    C. Miraculous Deliverance (3:19-30)

IV. Faithful Witness of God's Sovereignty (4:1-37)

    A. Nebuchadnezzar's Vision of a Tree (4:1-18)

    B. Daniel's Interpretation of the Vision (4:19-27)

    C. God Humbles Nebuchadnezzar (4:28-37)

V. Faithful Witness of God's Judgment (5:1-31)

    A. Belshazzar's Desecration of Holy Things (5:1-4)

    B. God's Handwriting on the Wall (5:5-6)

    C. Daniel's Interpretation of the Writing (5:7-29)

  D. Darius's Conquest of Babylon (5:30-31)

VI. Faithful Witness of God's Deliverance (6:1–28)

  A. The Character of Daniel (6:1-3)

  B. The Enemies of Daniel (6:4-9)

  C. The Courage of Daniel (6:10-11)

  D. The Punishment of Daniel (6:12-17)

  E. The Deliverance of Daniel (6:18-28)

VII. Faithful Witness of God's Kingdom (7:1-28)

  A. Daniel's Vision (7:1-14)

  B. The Interpretation of Daniel's Vision (7:15-28)

VIII. Faithful Witness of the Last Days (8:1-27)

  A. Daniel's Vision (8:1-14)

  B. The Interpretation of Daniel's Vision (8:15-27)

IX. Faithful Witness Through Prayer and Fasting (9:1-27)

  A. Daniel's Prayer and Confession (9:1-19)

  B. Gabriel's Message to Daniel (9:20-27)

X. Faithful Witness in Light of the End (10:1–12:13)

  A. Daniel's Awesome Vision (10:1–11:1)

  B. Prophecies Concerning the Nations (11:2-5)

  C. Prophecies Concerning the End of Days (12:1-13)

A Chronology of Daniel's Times

609 BC	Jehoiakim begins to reign in Jerusalem as king over Judah.
606 BC	Daniel and other leaders are taken captive and deported to Babylon (Daniel 1).
598 BC	King Jehoiachin reigns over Judah. Nebuchadnezzar invades Judah again and takes more people to Babylon.
595 BC	Nebuchadnezzar's first dream (Daniel 2).

588 BC	Nebuchadnezzar destroys Jerusalem and the Temple. He exiles most of the population of Judah to Babylon.
553 BC	Belshazzar rules in place of his father. Daniel's first vision (Daniel 7).
550 BC	Daniel's second vision (Daniel 8).
539 BC	Medo-Persians conquer Babylon (Daniel 5).
539 BC	Daniel is thrown to the lions (Daniel 6).
539 BC	Daniel's third vision (Daniel 9).
539 BC	Decree of Cyrus, king of Persia, allowing the Jews to return to Jerusalem.
538 BC	Foundation is laid for rebuilding the Temple in Jerusalem.
537 BC	Daniel's fourth vision (Daniel 10–12).

major profits had longer books than minor profits - that's only difference

INTRODUCTION
to an Inductive Study of Daniel

Why Study Daniel?

What does it mean to be a believer in the midst of an unbelieving world? How can we live out our faith when we are not in power? How can we remain faithful to God when we are surrounded by other religions and systems of belief? Throughout history, Christians have struggled with these questions. The Book of Daniel answers these questions and more. Daniel speaks to the challenge of being in the world but not of the world (see John 17:16). Even in the Old Testament, the people of God were oppressed and opposed by the powers of this world. We read that Daniel was captured by the Babylonian army and was taken to Babylon, where he and the Jewish people suffered seventy years of exile. They lost their land and their liberty; they were robbed of their rights; and they struggled to survive under the rule of Babylonian tyrants.

In these ten Bible study lessons, we will be reading and discovering the Book of Daniel, and we will learn how to trust God in the midst of challenging times. As we stated above, the Book of Daniel can be divided into two parts. The first part (chapters 1–6) contains stories about Daniel and his Hebrew friends, in which the kings of Babylon threaten to bring the faithful Jews to an end. In each case, however, God overrules the human rulers with amazing interventions that protect the Hebrews. The second part of the book (chapters 7–12) contains visions of the end that unveil the deeper dimensions of God's present and future sovereign rule. The visions show that just as God ruled over the life and times of Daniel, God continues to rule over every earthly kingdom. Ultimately, God will bring all human kingdoms to an end, and He will establish His eternal kingdom with Jesus the Messiah as King.

The visions of Daniel are similar to the visions of John in the Book of Revelation, and the two books have a similar purpose. Visions of the end give us a broad picture of the future, but they are not designed to be a detailed calendar of events. I would like to say that this study will answer all your questions about the Book of Daniel; but, unfortunately, that is not the case. Dedicated and intelligent Bible scholars have wrestled with Daniel's prophecies for over 2000 years, and they have not reached agreement on the meaning of all the details. As I studied prominent prophecy teachers (such as Clarence Larkin, C.I. Scofield, Finis Dake, and Tim LaHaye), I was surprised to learn that their interpretations of Daniel do not always agree. The purpose of an "inductive Bible study" is to learn as much as possible about the biblical text at hand—in this case, the Book of Daniel. Therefore, we will attempt to keep our interpretations as close as possible to the words of Daniel himself, without spending too much time in Matthew 24 or in the Book of Revelation, which did not exist in Daniel's day.

Although Daniel's prophecies still retain some mystery, his visions assure us that God is in control and that we can trust in Him. The visions of the end give us vibrant hope so that we can fulfill our mission as faithful witnesses of Jesus Christ until he returns. Even in the face of difficult challenges and persecution, we can live faithfully in the light of the end, as we look for the "blessed hope and glorious appearing of our great God and Savior Jesus Christ" (Titus 2:13 NKJV).

Your Inductive Bible Study

From the start, we need to understand that we will be using a special method for studying the Bible. Rather than simply being told what Daniel means, you will be taught how to discover God's Word for yourself. This method is called *inductive Bible study*. The word *inductive* means "to be drawn into." So, through the use of carefully prepared steps, you will be drawn into the meaning of the Book of Daniel. These steps are:

       1. **DISCOVER**   (*observation*)

       2. **DISCERN**   (*interpretation*)

       3. **DEVOTE**   (*commitment and obedience*)

       4. **DISCIPLE**   (*application*)

The guidance of the Holy Spirit is essential in this method of studying the Bible. Indeed, the Scriptures say that the Holy Spirit will lead us to all truth (John 16:13). This is the heart of inductive Bible study. The Holy Spirit leads or draws us into the truth of God's Word.

Throughout this entire study, you will encounter sections titled Pause for Prayer. Here you will be invited to pray about each of the four steps of inductive study as described above. In prayer, you can ask the Holy Spirit to grant you wisdom and understanding (Colossians 1:9) so that you might rightly divide the Word of truth (2 Timothy 2:15). The pause for prayer sections are really mini-devotions that are designed to help you encounter God as you study His Word.

Let's take a closer look at each of the four steps of inductive Bible study. This will help you apply these steps in a way that will lead to a sound and informed interpretation of each passage in Daniel.

STEP 1—DISCOVER

Observation: The active learning principle here is *observation*. The Discover step asks the question, *What do I see in this passage*? The goal of this step is to discover the central facts contained in the Scriptures. Specially designed questions will aid you in prying out the details found in the section being studied. These questions are called Helping Questions. They basically ask: Who? What? When? Where? Why? and How? In answering the Helping Questions, you will begin to see the central elements contained in the passage. Also, after answering the Helping Questions, you will be given the opportunity to make some of your own. In this way you will begin to see even more facts contained in the Bible.

Remember that inductive Bible study is not meant to be a dry gathering of Bible facts. Rather, inductive study is a process whereby one becomes formed and transformed by God's Word and the power of the Holy Spirit.

The Pause for Prayer sections can help you along this spiritual journey as you study the Bible inductively. As you work through the Discover section take full advantage of the Pause for Prayer by asking the Holy Spirit to reveal to you what is contained in the Bible. Pray that the Spirit quickens your powers of observation so that you will be well-prepared to go on to the next steps of inductive study.

STEP 2—DISCERN

Interpretation: The active learning principle here is *interpretation*. The Discern step asks the question, *What does this passage mean*? The goal of this step is not just to uncover facts, but rather to gain real understanding into what the passage means. The method for obtaining a deeper meaning of the text is by using helping tools.

This is the most fun and creative part of inductive Bible study! Helping tools consist of creating symbols, markings, highlighting, underlining and the like to note special words, phrases, and patterns in the Scripture. As you develop these helping tools, key terms, patterns, emphases, and repetitions will become evident in the text.

You will want to make helping tools that clearly communicate to you personally. For example, every time you see a reference to the sacrifice of Christ you might want to draw a cross. Similarly, when you encounter a reference to the Holy Spirit, you might want to put in a small image of a dove.

Note some additional symbols and markings that you might choose to use in your inductive Bible study.

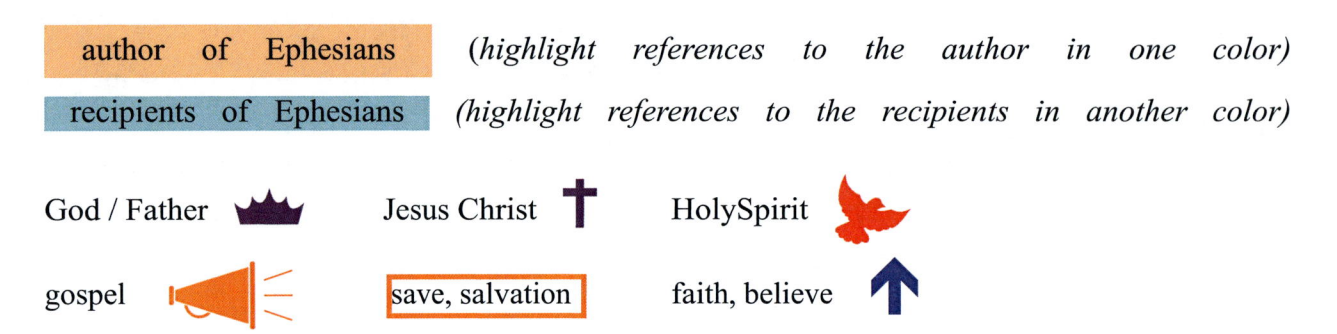

author of Ephesians (highlight references to the author in one color)

recipients of Ephesians (highlight references to the recipients in another color)

God / Father ♛   Jesus Christ ✝   HolySpirit 🕊

gospel 📣   save, salvation (boxed)   faith, believe ⬆

The options in the Discern step are limited only by your own imagination. However, once you choose a symbol, color, or marking element, be consistent in its use. In this way, every time you see the symbol of the cross, you will immediately know that some aspect of Christ's sacrifice is being spoken of. ***Discerning what the Bible says.*** Once you have finished marking the text with your helping tools, you will want to step back and examine your work. What patterns, repetitions, and emphases have emerged? Pray that God will show you the meaning of patterns and special words. Go back and read through your Helping Questions and combine them with what the helping tools have revealed.

At this point, you might want to make reference to some Bible study aids in arriving at your understanding of the passage being studied. These Bible helps consist of good commentaries, Bible dictionaries, and various translations of the Bible. This study guide will be using the *New American Standard Version* of the Bible (NASB) because it stays very close to the original wording of the Hebrew and Greek texts. However, other very good translations are the *King James Version* (KJV), the *New King James Version* (NKJV), and the *English Standard Version* (ESV). There are also some good online Bible study aids such as www.BibleGateway.com and www.BibleStudyTools.com. A number of helpful commentaries, dictionaries, and online sources are included at the end of this lesson.

The really powerful part of inductive study is not just knowing what the Bible means, but rather knowing what the Bible means for you personally. The Devote step of inductive study is designed to help you hear God's voice through what you have learned.

STEP 3—DEVOTE

Commitment and Obedience: The important aspects of the Devote step are commitment and obedience. The Devote step asks the question, *What does God want me to do in light of everything that I have learned from this passage of Scripture?* This is where real discipleship begins on a personal level. Prayer, reflection, and communion with the Holy Spirit are of upmost importance in the Devote step. This is where you ask God to open your heart to His perfect will in your life as it has been expressed in the passage you have just studied. Again, the pause for prayer section can help you enter into that spiritual realm to hear God's personal word for your life. Carefully crafted questions will help you to enter into a deeper level of commitment and obedience to the Bible. You will be invited to develop your own questions to ask God as you continue on your path to discipleship. Such questions might include:

- What does God expect me to do in light of what I have learned?
- Is God calling me to repentance through His Word?
- Is He wanting me to receive forgiveness, or perhaps what is more important, to give forgiveness?
- Does God want me to grow in faith and trust in Him?
- Is God calling me to a new aspect of ministry?

The Devote step is the most deeply personal part of inductive Bible study. Yet in a real way, it is the most important part of your study. The Devote step is a call to take all that you have learned and to put it into action in your personal life. The Devote step prays to God to make a real difference in your life in how you view Him, yourself, and others. The Devote step seeks the power of the Holy Spirit to actualize God's will in your daily life—the central theme of Daniel.

As you prayerfully work through the Devote step, you might want to jot down some notes or make more formal entries in your journal. In this way, you can return to these important moments in your *path to faithful witness*.

STEP 4—DISCIPLE

Application: The important idea of the Disciple step is *application*. The Disciple step is a call to action. Specifically, it is a personal challenge to take clear steps in living out your new commitments to God.

In a real sense, the Disciple step is taking all that you have learned in your inductive study, together with your newfound commitments to God, and walking in the Spirit (Romans 8:1–4).

The Disciple step involves stepping out in faith and in the power of the Holy Spirit to take concrete action on God's Word. If the Discover step addresses your head (*What are the facts contained in this passage?*) and the Devote step addresses your heart (*What is God saying to me personally in this passage?*), the Disciple step addresses your hands (*What does God actually want me to do in light of this passage?*). This is why the Disciple step will present you with some fairly direct challenges in the form of, "*This week I commit to....*"

The Disciple step does not stop with our own spiritual development. It is an opportunity for us to obey the Great Commission of our Lord and make disciples for Him. As we continually grow through the inductive study of the Bible, we can seek out others to influence for the Lord. We can pray that the Lord will use us to disciple others for Him and to enhance their service in His kingdom.

Some Practical Tips for Doing Inductive Bible Study

You will first want to read the key verse at the beginning of each lesson of your study. While reflecting upon the key verse, you will want to prepare your heart by prayerfully reading through the Pause for Prayer. Then, you will carefully read through the actual text for that lesson. This is to be an active reading whereby you zone in on the words and concepts that are present in your section of Scripture. After you have a good orientation to your reading, you will begin to work through each of the four steps of inductive study: **Discover, Discern, Devote,** and **Disciple.**

As you continue through each step, take careful note of what you are being asked to do. For example, you will be asked to answer leading questions, develop a marking system for the text, write out your own questions, and the like. Be careful and consistent in how you respond to the expectations presented in each lesson. All of this is to be immersed in prayer and sensitivity to the guidance of the Holy Spirit. If you are completing your inductive study as part of a group, you should be prepared to share some of your findings with others. This will require you to be prepared in advance and be familiar with the lesson under discussion. Keep in mind that your journey through the Bible can be of great help to others in their walk with the Lord. In fact, this is a vital part of the Disciple step of inductive study.

Although a major goal of inductive study is that you discover God's Word for yourself, this does not mean that you cannot seek help in interpreting the Bible. That is why a list of commentaries and Bible study helps are provided below.

Before you begin your study of Daniel, we want to extend a special word of thanks to you for choosing *Daniel: A Path to Faithful Witness*. It is our prayer that you be truly transformed by your experience.

Helpful Supplies and Resources

GUIDELINES FOR INDUCTIVE STUDY

William A. Simmons, *Enliven: Encountering God through His Word*, Church of God Adult Discipleship, 2014. (The QR Code to the right links to the Adult Discipleship Department, where Simmons' book can be purchased.)

COMMENTARIES ON THE BOOK OF DANIEL

Robert A. Anderson, *Signs and wonders: A Commentary on the Book of Daniel*. Eerdmans, 1984).
Link to purchase: http://a.co/d/89qiat5

Paul R. House, *Daniel: An Introduction and Commentary*. IVP Academic, 2018.
Link to purchase: http://a.co/d/1qtat4b

Dale Ralph Davis, *The Message of Daniel*. IVP Academic, 2013. **Link to Purchase:** http://a.co/d/9qvGvAV

BIBLE DICTIONARIES, ENCYCLOPEDIAS, AND WORD STUDIES

J. D. Douglas and Merrill C. Tenney. *Zondervan Illustrated Bible Dictionary*, 2011.

James Strong. *The New Strong's Expanded Exhaustive Concordance of the Bible*, 2010.
Easton's Bible Dictionary: https://www.biblestudytools.com/dictionaries/eastons-bible-dictionary/ (The QR Code at right links to Easton's Bible Dictionary.)

The Jewish Encyclopedia: http://www.jewishencyclopedia.com (This QR Code links to the Jewish Encyclopedia Online.)

ONLINE SOURCES

Blue Letter Bible: www.blueletterbible.org/

BibleStudyTools.com: www.biblestudytools.com
Bible Hub: https://biblehub.com (The QR Code at right links to BibleHub.)

Enliven Encountering God Through His Word

LESSON ONE

DANIEL
1:1-21

FAITHFUL WITNESS IN CHALLENGING TIMES

Lesson One

DANIEL 1:1-21   1

LESSON ONE

DANIEL 1:1-21

Faithful Witness in Challenging Times

🗝 KEY

But Daniel made up his mind that he would not defile himself with the king's choice food or with the wine which he drank; so he sought permission from the commander of the officials that he might not defile himself (Daniel 1:8).

Introduction

If you are already familiar with the inductive Bible study method, you are well on your way to discovering God's Word for yourself. However, if this is your first inductive Bible study, you are starting a life-giving and exciting pathway. Each step of the way will lead you to new insights regarding the Scripture, new understandings of the Christian life, and new commitments in your walk with God. Hopefully, you will walk this pathway of inductive Bible study for the rest of your life.

This guide to the Book of Daniel will lead you through the essential steps of inductive study. The Helping Questions will assist you in learning the many facts contained in the passage. Your development of helping tools (making special symbols, highlighting, underlining, etc.) will reveal special features about the text, such as comparisons, contrasts, parallels, and more. There is no need for you to memorize the various aspects of inductive Bible study, because this guide will remind you of each step. If you simply follow the guidelines on each page, do the exercises, and participate in group discussions, the message of the Book of Daniel will emerge for you. Do not be overly concerned about getting the answers "right." Many of the questions are open-ended and could have a variety of good answers. Inductive Bible study is a "hands-on" process, whereby the students learn the Bible for themselves.

1 Lesson One

This means that when you have finished *Daniel: A Path to Faithful Witness*, you will have developed several helpful tools that you can use every time you open the Bible. Also, by carefully answering the Who? What? When? Where? Why? and How? Helping Questions, you will have developed your own comments and insights into the Book of Daniel. Perhaps most important is that by the end of your study on Daniel, you will have faithfully responded to the Devote and Disciple steps of inductive study. Since these steps not only require personal commitment to God's Word but also encourage you to take concrete action in response to God's Word, you will have developed into a more mature and informed believer. This is the goal of discipleship—putting God's Word into action in our personal lives.

The format of this student guide to the Book of Daniel will follow the same pattern in each of the ten chapters. This repetition of steps is designed to implant good Bible study habits and to instill in you the confidence to continue your study of the Scripture. Furthermore, by encountering the same sequence of steps in each lesson, you will always know what is coming next. At the same time, being "drawn into" (the literal meaning of *inductive*) the Bible is never to be a routine or mechanical exercise. Therefore, your study of Daniel should be covered in prayer, so the Holy Spirit will guide your thoughts and reveal the truth to you. The sections titled Pause for Prayer are carefully designed devotions that will help you prepare your mind and heart to receive the message of God's Word. Before going any further, let us pause for prayer!

Pause for Prayer

At the beginning of this first lesson, let us take time to pray for the entire study of Daniel. "Open my eyes, that I may behold wondrous things out of your law" (Psalm 119:18 ESV). Lord God, we ask You to open our spiritual eyes to show us the glimpses of glory we cannot see by ourselves. "The natural person does not accept the things of the Spirit of God, for they are folly to him, and he is not able to understand them because they are spiritually discerned" (1 Corinthians 2:14 ESV). Help us by Your Spirit, that we may discern the spiritual meaning of the Book of Daniel. Give us this spiritual sight and the gift of seeing "wondrous things" in Your Word. We ask that You make our hearts warm and soft and that our study of Daniel will prevent us from growing cold. We praise You and thank You for speaking to us as we study. In the wonderful name of Jesus, we pray. Amen.

DANIEL 1:1-21   1

THE TEXT

Daniel 1:1-21 NASB 1995

¹ In the third year of the reign of Jehoiakim king of Judah, Nebuchadnezzar king of Babylon came to Jerusalem and besieged it. ² The Lord gave Jehoiakim king of Judah into his hand, along with some of the vessels of the house of God; and he brought them to the land of Shinar, to the house of his god, and he brought the vessels into the treasury of his god.

³ Then the king ordered Ashpenaz, the chief of his officials, to bring in some of the sons of Israel, including some of the royal family and of the nobles, ⁴ youths in whom was no defect, who were good-looking, showing intelligence in every *branch of* wisdom, endowed with understanding and discerning knowledge, and who had ability for serving in the king's court; and *he ordered him* to teach them the literature and language of the Chaldeans. ⁵ The king appointed for them a daily ration from the king's choice food and from the wine which he drank, and *appointed* that they should be educated three years, at the end of which they were to enter the king's personal service. ⁶ Now among them from the sons of Judah were Daniel, Hananiah, Mishael and Azariah. ⁷ Then the commander of the officials assigned *new* names to them; and to Daniel he assigned *the name* Belteshazzar, to Hananiah Shadrach, to Mishael Meshach and to Azariah Abed-nego.

⁸ But Daniel made up his mind that he would not defile himself with the king's choice food or with the wine which he drank; so he sought *permission* from the commander of the officials that he might not defile himself. ⁹ Now God granted Daniel favor and compassion in the sight of the commander of

Lesson One

the officials, ¹⁰ and the commander of the officials said to Daniel, "I am afraid of my lord the king, who has appointed your food and your drink; for why should he see your faces looking more haggard than the youths who are your own age? Then you would make me forfeit my head to the king." ¹¹ But Daniel said to the overseer whom the commander of the officials had appointed over Daniel, Hananiah, Mishael and Azariah, ¹² "Please test your servants for ten days, and let us be given some vegetables to eat and water to drink. ¹³ Then let our appearance be observed in your presence and the appearance of the youths who are eating the king's choice food; and deal with your servants according to what you see."

¹⁴ So he listened to them in this matter and tested them for ten days. ¹⁵ At the end of ten days their appearance seemed better and they were fatter than all the youths who had been eating the king's choice food. ¹⁶ So the overseer continued to withhold their choice food and the wine they were to drink, and kept giving them vegetables.

¹⁷ As for these four youths, God gave them knowledge and intelligence in every *branch of* literature and wisdom; Daniel even understood all *kinds of* visions and dreams.

¹⁸ Then at the end of the days which the king had specified for presenting them, the commander of the officials presented them before Nebuchadnezzar. ¹⁹ The king talked with them, and out of them all not one was found like Daniel, Hananiah, Mishael and Azariah; so they entered the king's personal service. ²⁰ As for every matter of wisdom and understanding about which the king consulted them, he found them ten times better than all the magicians *and* conjurers who *were* in all his realm. ²¹ And Daniel continued until the first year of Cyrus the king.

DANIEL 1:1-21   1

Discover

The focus of the Discover step is to uncover the facts contained in the passage we are studying. These facts will be revealed to you as you answer the questions: Who? What? When? Where? and How? All the facts that you discover will feed into your interpretation later. Reread Daniel 1:1-21 and answer the sample Helping Questions below.

Sample Helping Questions

1. The first chapter of Daniel introduces us to the whole book. It tells us about Daniel and his friends, and it explains why they were in Babylon. Starting with the basics, make a list of the people in Daniel 1, and briefly describe each person.

   Jeho
   _____
   _____
   _____
   _____

2. Summarize the main events in the story in Daniel 1.

   _____
   _____
   _____
   _____

3. What reasons would Nebuchadnezzar have for taking all the vessels from the Temple in Jerusalem and placing them in his Babylonian temple? Does Nebuchadnezzar have any respect for the God of Israel?

   _____
   _____
   _____
   _____
   _____

1 Lesson One

4. The name *Daniel* means "God is my judge," and *Mishael* means "Who is like God." *Hananiah* means "Jehovah is gracious," and *Azariah* means "Jehovah is my helper." Why would Babylonian names be given to the Hebrew captives?

   _____
   _____
   _____
   _____

5. Why did Daniel not want to eat the king's food? What is the meaning of the word "defile?" What kind of risk was Daniel taking in refusing to obey the king?

   _____
   _____
   _____
   _____

Create some of Your Helping Questions that will enable you to Discover the treasures that can be found in Daniel chapter 1.

Your Helping Questions

_____
_____
_____
_____
_____
_____
_____
_____

Daniel 1:1-21

Your Helping Questions have discovered many more facts in Daniel 1:1-21. Here are a few more questions that you may not have come to mind. Consider these additional questions now.

1. What is the role of God in this story? That is, what does God do for the Hebrew captives?

Lesson One

2. Why were the Israelites taken into captivity? Was their exile a judgment from God? (Read 2 Kings 23:36–25:24.)

_____
_____
_____
_____
_____

Discern

The Discern step employs a number of helping tools. The helping tools consist of underlining, highlighting, making special symbols, etc. All these marking systems will reveal patterns in the biblical text. These patterns include parallel thoughts, contrasts, repetitions, and the like. For example, if you use the symbol of a crown to represent God, and you find yourself drawing the crown throughout the passage, you will see how the activity of God is present in the story.

Concentrate on being creative when working through the Discern step. Make up symbols or marking systems that are meaningful for you. Keep track of these symbols and color-coding so that you can reuse the same system throughout each lesson in this study guide. In this way, you will become so familiar with your own scheme of marking a text that you will be able to notice important themes at a glance. You should make up new ways of marking the text as the subject requires, but be ready to carry over tried and true symbols that you have used in past lessons. In no time, you will have a good number of familiar ways of marking any section of the Bible.

For example, you might notice the word "wisdom" is stated more than once. Several synonyms and related words are also used. Mark each place that "wisdom" and related words occur in Daniel 1. Wisdom is often associated with the Holy Spirit. Can you find scriptures that speak about the relationship between wisdom and the Spirit? Also, you might observe the progress of Daniel's leadership as the story develops. Does his prominence in the story seem to be connected to his righteous character?

Pause for Prayer

O Lord, our hearts are filled with gratitude for Your Word. Our appreciation for the power of the Word was captured long ago by the psalmist who wrote these words:

DANIEL 1:1-21   1

The law of the Lord is perfect, converting the soul;

The testimony of the Lord is sure, making wise the simple;

The statutes of the Lord are right, rejoicing the heart;

The commandment of the Lord is pure, enlightening the eyes;

The fear of the Lord is clean, enduring forever;

The judgments of the Lord are true and righteous altogether.

More to be desired are they than gold, Yea, than much fine gold;

Sweeter also than honey and the honeycomb.

Moreover by them Your servant is warned,

And in keeping them there is great reward.

Who can understand his errors? Cleanse me from secret faults.

Keep back Your servant also from presumptuous sins;

Let them not have dominion over me.

Then I shall be blameless, And I shall be innocent of great transgression.

Let the words of my mouth and the meditation of my heart

Be acceptable in Your sight, O Lord, my strength and my Redeemer

(Psalm 19:7-14 NKJV).

We ask these things in the name of our Lord Jesus Christ. Amen.

→ PULLING IT ALL TOGETHER ←

You have already observed many of the facts in Daniel 1 by way of the Helping Questions. Also, your helping tools have revealed many of the features and patterns contained in this passage. At this point, you should review all your answers to the Helping Questions and what you have discerned by way of your helping tools and summarize everything below.

1. Summarize what you learned regarding repeated words and phrases.

___

___

___

Lesson One

2. Explain the works of God that are revealed in Daniel 1. Consider the following: "the Lord gave ..." (verse 2); "God granted ..." (verse 9); and "God gave ..." (verse 17).

_____

_____

_____

_____

_____

3. In what way does Daniel's behavior demonstrate his faith in God in challenging times? How is Daniel's experience a good example of the truth found in James 1:12?

_____

_____

_____

_____

_____

You may want to consult with your Bible dictionaries or encyclopedias to learn more about Jehoiakim (king of Judah), Nebuchadnezzar (king of Babylon), Shinar (region around the Tigris and Euphrates rivers), the Chaldeans, and Cyrus (king of Persia). They can be found online here:

Jehoiakim, https://www.blueletterbible.org/search/Dictionary/viewTopic.cfm?topic=ET0002009

Nebuchadnezzar, https://www.blueletterbible.org/search/Dictionary/viewTopic.cfm?topic=ET0002684

Shinar, https://www.blueletterbible.org/search/Dictionary/viewTopic.cfm?topic=BT0003913

Chaldeans, https://www.blueletterbible.org/search/Dictionary/viewTopic.cfm?topic=BT0000919

Cyrus, https://www.blueletterbible.org/search/Dictionary/viewTopic.cfm?topic=BT0001105

Also, a map of the ancient Middle East can be found here:

https://www.blueletterbible.org/images/rosepub/imageDisplay/maps_ancient_b

DANIEL 1:1-21   1

Summarize Your Findings

_____

You can now put together everything that you have learned and write out your interpretation of this passage. Do not worry that your interpretation may be different from someone else's interpretation. There is more than one way of describing the teachings of this biblical text, and just the activity of putting your thoughts into words will help you remember the message of Daniel.

1 Lesson One

Your Interpretation

In this step, you will record your interpretations of this chapter of Daniel in the areas of Christian beliefs, practices, and spirituality. How does this biblical text inform our beliefs regarding the nature and character of God, the plans and purposes of God, the doctrines of salvation, sanctification, Holy Spirit, sin, healing, the last days, the family, the Church, etc.? Are there issues in this text that you do not understand or that cause you to be uncomfortable? Explain how this text may impact spiritual topics like prayer, fasting, witnessing, testimony, giving, study, worship, sacraments, etc. Write down any interpretations that relate to our beliefs, practices, or spirituality. You might notice in this chapter an emphasis on the judgment of God, the sovereignty of God, the faithfulness of God, the faith and dedication of Daniel, and the charismatic gifts of wisdom and interpretation.

DANIEL 1:1-21

Devote

In this step of our Bible study, you strengthen your relationship to God. It is not enough to read and study the Bible—we must devote ourselves to serving and worshiping the God of the Bible. It is time to allow the Holy Spirit to speak to you on a deeper level. Basically, you should ask, "God, in light of what You have taught me in Your Word, what do You want me to do?" As you enter into this Devote section, consider the following:

1. By now you have become very familiar with this chapter of Daniel. Therefore, you are ready to let the passage speak to your heart, if you have not already done so. In this step, you should write down the effect this passage has on you as a believer. How does it make you feel? What emotions are brought to the surface as you read the text? Do you feel gratitude, joy, hope, love, heaviness, conviction, guilt, liberty, awe, amazement, or courage?

   _____
   _____
   _____
   _____
   _____

2. Daniel and his friends chose to maintain a faithful witness even in the midst of a foreign land. The Scripture says that "Daniel made up his mind not to defile himself." What have you "made up your mind" to do in response to this text?

   _____
   _____
   _____
   _____
   _____
   _____

LESSON ONE

3. How has this text affected you? Are there situations where, like Daniel, you have been under pressure to conform to non-Christian attitudes and behavior? Do you sense a transformation of your heart? Do you desire a certain kind of transformation?

_____
_____
_____
_____
_____
_____
_____
_____
_____
_____
_____
_____

Pause for Prayer

At this point, you should pray that God will show you the areas of your life where you can become a better disciple of Jesus Christ. Write down anything that the Holy Spirit brings to your mind.

Then, pray this prayer: "Heavenly Father, as Jesus walked with the disciples on the road to Emmaus, he expounded to them all the Scriptures concerning Himself. As they reflected on their experience, they said to one another, 'Did not our heart burn within us while He talked with us on the road, and while He opened the Scriptures to us?' (Luke 24:27-32 NKJV) Now, Lord, make our hearts aflame with Your Holy Word, that we may be transformed into Your likeness, set apart, and fit for the Master's use. In Christ's name we pray. Amen."

DANIEL 1:1-21 | 1

✝ ✗ DISCIPLE

A disciple is a learner and a follower of Jesus Christ. The purpose of this inductive Bible study is to make us better disciples. Your study of Daniel 1 has already brought to your attention several areas where you can learn more and other areas where you can follow Jesus more closely. In this step that we call "Disciple," you should focus on the commitments that you can make, which will lead you forward on the *Path to Faithful Witness* in challenging times.

In light of what we have learned from Daniel 1:1-21, I would suggest the following commitments:

1. I will be faithful and obedient to Jesus Christ, so that I may not come under judgment.

2. I will resist the temptations of the Enemy, and I will refuse to compromise when placed under pressure.

3. I will trust God to make a way for me, to open doors, and to work miracles on my behalf.

4. I will rejoice in God's faithfulness.

5. I will rest in the knowledge that God is in control of my life, my circumstances, and my future.

6. I will glorify God with the material and spiritual gifts that God has given to me. I will step out by faith and allow God to use me in His work.

A good disciple will also *make disciples* of other people. The Great Commission tells us, "Go therefore and make disciples of all the nations" (Matthew 28:19). The responsibility for making disciples rests upon every one of us. Making disciples begins with being a good example to others, just as Daniel was (see also 1 Timothy 4:12). Making disciples also includes sharing with others what we have learned about serving God.

Through his faithful witness, Daniel was an influence upon everyone around him. Ask God to show you the ways that you can be a positive influence in your family, church, and community.

ENLIVEN ENCOUNTERING GOD Through HIS WORD

LESSON TWO

DANIEL
2:1-49

FAITHFUL WITNESS THROUGH THE HOLY SPIRIT

2 Lesson Two

DANIEL 2:1-49

LESSON TWO

Daniel 2:1-49

Faithful Witness Through the Holy Spirit

KEY VERSE

To You, O God of my fathers, I give thanks and praise, for You have given me wisdom and power; even now You have made known to me what we requested of You, for You have made known to us the king's matter (Daniel 2:23).

Introduction

We learned in Daniel 1:1 that Nebuchadnezzar was the Babylonian king who invaded Jerusalem and took the Hebrews to Babylon as his captives. There, Daniel and his friends were trained for three years in the language, literature, and religion of Babylon. In those days, Babylon was the most powerful nation on earth, and people probably thought it would endure forever. However, God gave Nebuchadnezzar a dream that showed the end of all human kingdoms. God will rule the earth, and the kingdom of Jesus Christ will endure forever.

Whenever God reveals the future, He does so for a purpose. God's revelations in the Book of Daniel will make us hopeful while trusting in God (Titus 2:13), patient while enduring trials in this present world (James 5:7-8), expectant while anticipating the coming of the end at any moment (1 Thessalonians 5:2-4), faithful while seeking a closer walk with God (1 John 3:2-3; 2 Peter 3:11-13), and diligent while knowing that we will be rewarded (1 Corinthians 15:58). Jesus came and proclaimed the coming of the kingdom of God, and the Holy Spirit works in us to create a longing for the Kingdom, a longing for God himself.

Without Daniel, Nebuchadnezzar would never have known the meaning of his dream; and without the Holy Spirit, Daniel would not have been able to understand the dream. When we are faced with an impossible situation, we can rely on the Holy Spirit to guide us into all truth (See John 14:26; 15:26-27).

2 Lesson Two

PAUSE for PRAYER

Let us pray as we prepare to enter the study of God's Word. The following prayer was written by Origen, one of the early Church Fathers. "Lord, inspire us to read your Scriptures and to meditate upon them day and night. We ask you to give us real understanding of what we need, that we, in turn, may put its precepts into practice. Yet we know that understanding and good intentions are fruitless, unless rooted in your graceful love. So we ask that the words of Scripture may also be not just signs on a page, but channels of grace into our hearts." In the wonderful name of Jesus, we pray. Amen.

THE TEXT

Daniel 2:1-49

¹Now in the second year of the reign of Nebuchadnezzar, Nebuchadnezzar had dreams; and his spirit was troubled and his sleep left him. ²Then the king gave orders to call in the magicians, the conjurers, the sorcerers and the Chaldeans to tell the king his dreams. So they came in and stood before the king. ³The king said to them, "I had a dream and my spirit is anxious to understand the dream."

⁴Then the Chaldeans spoke to the king in Aramaic: "O king, live forever! Tell the dream to your servants, and we will declare the interpretation." ⁵The king replied to the Chaldeans, "The command from me is firm: if you do not make known to me the dream and its interpretation, you will be ˡtorn limb from limb and your houses will be made a rubbish heap. ⁶But if you declare the dream and its interpretation, you will receive from me gifts and a reward and great honor; therefore declare to me the dream and its interpretation." ⁷They answered a second time and said, "Let the king tell the dream to his servants, and we will declare the interpretation." ⁸The king replied, "I know for certain that you

DANIEL 2:1-49   2

are bargaining for time, inasmuch as you have seen that the command from me is firm, ⁹that if you do not make the dream known to me, there is only one decree for you. For you have agreed together to speak lying and corrupt words before me until the situation is changed; therefore tell me the dream, that I may know that you can declare to me its interpretation." ¹⁰The Chaldeans answered the king and said, "There is not a man on earth who could declare the matter for the king, inasmuch as no great king or ruler has *ever* asked anything like this of any magician, conjurer or Chaldean. ¹¹Moreover, the thing which the king demands is difficult, and there is no one else who could declare it to the king except gods, whose dwelling place is not with *mortal* flesh."

¹²Because of this the king became indignant and very furious and gave orders to destroy all the wise men of Babylon. ¹³So the decree went forth that the wise men should be slain; and they looked for Daniel and his friends to kill *them*.

¹⁴Then Daniel replied with discretion and discernment to Arioch, the captain of the king's bodyguard, who had gone forth to slay the wise men of Babylon; ¹⁵he said to Arioch, the king's commander, "For what reason is the decree from the king *so* urgent?" Then Arioch informed Daniel about the matter. ¹⁶So Daniel went in and requested of the king that he would give him time, in order that he might declare the interpretation to the king.

¹⁷Then Daniel went to his house and informed his friends, Hananiah, Mishael and Azariah, about the matter, ¹⁸so that they might request compassion from the God of heaven concerning this mystery, so that Daniel and his friends would not be destroyed with the rest of the wise men of Babylon.

¹⁹Then the mystery was revealed to Daniel in a night vision. Then Daniel blessed the God of

2   Lesson Two

heaven; [20]Daniel said, "Let the name of God be blessed forever and ever, for wisdom and power belong to Him. [21] "It is He who changes the times and the epochs; He removes kings and establishes kings; He gives wisdom to wise men and knowledge to men of understanding. [22] "It is He who reveals the profound and hidden things; He knows what is in the darkness, and the light dwells with Him. [23] "To You, O God of my fathers, I give thanks and praise, for You have given me wisdom and power; even now You have made known to me what we requested of You, For You have made known to us the king's matter." [24] Therefore, Daniel went in to Arioch, whom the king had appointed to destroy the wise men of Babylon; he went and spoke to him as follows: "Do not destroy the wise men of Babylon! Take me into the king's presence, and I will declare the interpretation to the king."

[25] Then Arioch hurriedly brought Daniel into the king's presence and spoke to him as follows: "I have found a man among the exiles from Judah who can make the interpretation known to the king!" [26] The king said to Daniel, whose name was Belteshazzar, "Are you able to make known to me the dream which I have seen and its interpretation?" [27] Daniel answered before the king and said, "As for the mystery about which the king has inquired, neither wise men, conjurers, magicians *nor* diviners are able to declare *it* to the king. [28] However, there is a God in heaven who reveals mysteries, and He has made known to King Nebuchadnezzar what will take place in the latter days. This was your dream and the visions in your mind *while* on your bed. [29] As for you, O king, *while* on your bed your thoughts [turned to what would take place in the future; and He who reveals mysteries has made known to you what will take place. [30] But as for me, this mystery has not been revealed to me for any wisdom residing in me more than *in* any *other* living man, but for the purpose of making the interpretation known to the king, and that you may understand the thoughts of your mind.

The King's Dream

DANIEL 2:1-49 — **2**

[31] "You, O king, were looking and behold, there was a single great statue; that statue, which was large and of extraordinary splendor, was standing in front of you, and its appearance was awesome. [32] The head of that statue *was made* of fine gold, its breast and its arms of silver, its belly and its thighs of bronze, [33] its legs of iron, its feet partly of iron and partly of clay. [34] You continued looking until a stone was cut out without hands, and it struck the statue on its feet of iron and clay and crushed them. [35] Then the iron, the clay, the bronze, the silver and the gold were crushed all at the same time and became like chaff from the summer threshing floors; and the wind carried them away so that not a trace of them was found. But the stone that struck the statue became a great mountain and filled the whole earth.

[36] "This *was* the dream; now we will tell its interpretation before the king. [37] You, O king, are the king of kings, to whom the God of heaven has given the kingdom, the power, the strength and the glory; [38] and wherever the sons of men dwell, *or* the beasts of the field, or the birds of the sky, He has given *them* into your hand and has caused you to rule over them all. **You are the head of gold.**

[39] After you there will arise another kingdom inferior to you, then another third kingdom of bronze, which will rule over all the earth.

[40] Then there will be a fourth kingdom as strong as iron; inasmuch as iron crushes and shatters all things, so, like iron that breaks in

GOLD
SILVER
BRONZE
IRON
IRON AND CLAY

NEBUCHADNEZZAR'S DREAM

Lesson Two

pieces, it will crush and break all these in pieces. ⁴¹ In that you saw the feet and toes, partly of potter's clay and partly of iron, it will be a divided kingdom; but it will have in it the toughness of iron, inasmuch as you saw the iron mixed with common clay. ⁴² As the toes of the feet *were* partly of iron and partly of pottery, *so* some of the kingdom will be strong and part of it will be brittle. ⁴³ And in that you saw the iron mixed with common clay, they will combine with one another ⁽in the seed of men; but they will not adhere to one another, even as iron does not combine with pottery.

⁴⁴ In the days of those kings the God of heaven will set up a kingdom which will never be destroyed, and *that* kingdom will not be left for another people; it will crush and put an end to all these kingdoms, but it will itself endure forever. ⁴⁵ Inasmuch as you saw that a stone was cut out of the mountain without hands and that it crushed the iron, the bronze, the clay, the silver and the gold, the great God has made known to the king what will take place in the future; so the dream is true and its interpretation is trustworthy."

⁴⁶ Then King Nebuchadnezzar fell on his face and did homage to Daniel, and gave orders to present to him an offering and fragrant incense. ⁴⁷ The king answered Daniel and said, "Surely your God is a God of gods and a Lord of kings and a revealer of mysteries, since you have been able to reveal this mystery." ⁴⁸ Then the king promoted Daniel and gave him many great gifts, and he made him ruler over the whole province of Babylon and chief prefect over all the wise men of Babylon. ⁴⁹ And Daniel made request of the king, and he appointed Shadrach, Meshach and Abed-nego over the administration of the province of Babylon, while Daniel *was* at the king's court.

DANIEL 2:1-49

2

Discover

It is significant that Nebuchadnezzar's dream was given near the beginning of his 43-year reign. Ancient kings were most vulnerable and their kingdoms were most unstable at the beginning, before they had proven themselves and solidified their support base. The dream is important because ancient Near Eastern peoples believed that God communicated His will through dreams.

Ancient kings had many advisors who would provide counsel and direction. In this case, the king's advisors are listed in four categories: magicians, astrologers, sorcerers, and Chaldeans. Magicians were priests who were skilled at interpreting dreams. Astrologers interpreted a variety of signs in the stars, and they conjured spells to influence the future. Sorcerers were skilled in charms and incantations. The word "Chaldeans" encompasses all of the categories of wise men. Chaldeans were an ethnic group, but they were also diviners who explained mysteries and cast spells. These four categories overlapped in meaning, and the listing of all four indicates that the king called upon the leading wise men from every category of advisors.

When God gave Daniel the interpretation of the dream, Daniel's immediate response was to praise God with a song of thanksgiving (verses 20-23). After worshiping the Lord, Daniel notified Arioch that he was ready to disclose to the king the interpretation of his dream. Arioch brings Daniel to the king and seems to take credit for finding someone who will interpret the king's dream. The reference to Daniel as one of the captives from Judah reminds us of his status in the Babylonian kingdom. Daniel is an outsider from the lowest strata of society, but God honors his faith and uses him for His glory.

Sample Helping Questions

The following guidelines will help you discover the facts contained in this chapter of Daniel.

1. Read chapter 2 of Daniel straight through in order to gain an overall picture of the content and message of the passage. List the main events of this passage.

   What happens in verse 1?

   _____

   _____

   _____

2 Lesson Two

    What happens in verses 2-12?

    What happens in verses 13-16?

    What happens in verses 17-24?

    What happens in verses 25-45?

    What happens in verses 46-49?

2. What was the king's unreasonable request, and what means did he use to get what he wanted?

DANIEL 2:1-49

3. Daniel's approach to Arioch was discreet and tactful. What does this say about Daniel's ability to act with wisdom even in a difficult situation?

4. This passage is the first reference to prayer in the Book of Daniel, but it will not be the last. What is the significance of prayer in relation to Daniel's circumstances? Why does he pray? How does he pray? Why does he call upon his friends?

3. Throughout this passage, the revelation of the dream and its interpretation is called a "mystery," which is the Persian word *raz*. It refers to secret things that are hidden. Later Jewish writers used *raz* to signify things that can be known only by divine revelation. How many times does the word "mystery" occur in chapter 2? How does God reveal His "mysteries" to us today?

Lesson Two

4. What is Daniel's description of the statue in the dream? Write down the descriptive words that Daniel uses.

5. The statue is divided into different types of materials. The head of gold represents king Nebuchadnezzar. Other parts of the statue are not explained in terms of kings or kingdoms, but more information will be supplied in Daniel 7–12. Some Bible scholars identify the four kingdoms as Babylon, Medo-Persia, Greece, and Rome; but others believe they are Babylon, Media, Persia, and Greece. Why do you think these kingdoms are not named?

6. Whose kingdom is established after the rock crushes the statue? How long does this final kingdom last (see verse 44)?

Create some of your own Helping Questions that will enable you to Discover the treasures that can be found in Daniel chapter 2.

Your Helping Questions

2 Lesson Two

Your own Helping Questions have discovered many more facts in Daniel 1:1-21. Here are a few more questions that may not have come to mind. Consider these additional questions now.

1. What do you think is significant in Daniel's response to Arioch and to the king in verses 14-16?

2. What is noteworthy about God's response to Daniel's prayer (verse 19)?

3. What do verses 20-23 reveal about Daniel's perspective on the situation?

4. What are the most important points that Daniel makes to the king in verses 27-30?

DANIEL 2:1-49

5. What does verse 24 say to us about Daniel's character?

DISCERN

Daniel informs his three friends of the situation, and they pray for God to have compassion on them and reveal the secret so that they would not be killed. The inclusion of the three friends reminds us of the importance of community. We are part of the body of Christ, and we must stand together in times of testing.

The stone that is cut out without hands represents Jesus the Messiah, and He will strike the statue and destroy the human kingdoms. At that point, God will establish His eternal kingdom. All the human kingdoms come to an end, and God's kingdom fills the entire earth, replacing all previous human rule.

Daniel concludes his interpretation by declaring that the "dream is certain, and the interpretation thereof is sure." There must be no doubt that God rules and reigns, and His plan of redemption will be fulfilled.

The king was overwhelmed by the interpretation of the dream, and he fell on his face before Daniel to honor him. He also gave rewards to Daniel. Nebuchadnezzar proclaimed that Daniel's God was the "God of gods, the Lord of kings, and a revealer of secrets" (2:47 NKJV). This was a sincere and significant confession, but it falls short of our belief that Jehovah is the only God. In the ancient world, most cultures worshiped many gods. The Hebrew belief in only one God was a radical departure from the common polytheistic view of the surrounding peoples. Similarly, we must guard against idolatry in our own lives and in the Church (see Colossians 3:5). Jesus warned that we cannot serve two masters. We must examine ourselves and ask, "Which master do we serve?"

As a further reward, the king gave Daniel authority over the other wise men and over the whole province of Babylon. Given his newly acquired favor, Daniel requested of the king that Shadrach, Meshach, and Abed-nego be promoted also.

This Discern step brings to light patterns, a focal point, and repetitions that might otherwise go unnoticed. Review some of the symbols and marking systems that you used in Lesson One and see if you

LESSON TWO

can apply them here in Lesson Two. Do not be afraid to be creative in your invention of helping tools.

Before going any further, let us take a moment to seek for the guidance of the Holy Spirit as we study.

PAUSE for PRAYER

O Lord, our God, we pray for wisdom that we might discern Your message to us from Daniel chapter 2. Send your Holy Spirit to guide our thoughts as we listen to the biblical text. We come to this study with the attitude of the psalmist, who wrote these words:

> Blessed are the undefiled in the way, who walk in the law of the LORD!
>
> Blessed are those who keep His testimonies, who seek Him with the whole heart!
>
> They also do no iniquity; they walk in His ways.
>
> You have commanded us to keep Your precepts diligently.
>
> Oh, that my ways were directed to keep Your statutes!
>
> Then I would not be ashamed, when I look into all Your commandments.
>
> I will praise You with uprightness of heart, when I learn Your righteous judgments.
>
> I will keep Your statutes; Oh, do not forsake me utterly!" (Psalm 119:1-8 NKJV).

In the wonderful name of Jesus, we pray. Amen.

→PULLING IT ALL TOGETHER←

God revealed the mystery to Daniel so that the king might have understanding of the thoughts of his heart, thoughts concerning the future (verse 29). Apparently, the king had been thinking about his own future before he fell asleep. Then, after falling asleep, God gave him a dream that explained his future and what would come later.

The meaning of the statue will be further explained in Daniel 7, but we can summarize its historical sequence at this point. The head of gold is the Babylonian kingdom of Nebuchadnezzar. The arms and chest of silver are the Medo-Persian Empire. The belly and thighs of bronze represent the Greek Empire, and the legs of iron are the Roman Empire. During the time of the Roman Empire, Jesus appears on the scene, proclaiming that "the kingdom of heaven is at hand" (Matthew 4:17). With the coming of Jesus, the kingdom of God begins to grow until it fills the entire earth. The connection between the

DANIEL 2:1-49

rock and Jesus Christ is established through the following biblical texts: Psalm 118:22; Isaiah 8:14; Matthew 21:42; Mark 12:10-11; Luke 20:17-18; Romans 9:33; 1 Peter 2:6-8. Jesus is the stone that crushes all opponents (Luke 20:18). The dream reveals "what shall be in the latter days," a phrase that is normally taken as a reference to the end times, just as in Hosea 3:5; Isaiah 2:2; and Daniel 10:14.

The following questions may help you to summarize your findings:

1. Read verses 25-29 again. Who was the source of the king's dream?

2. Did Daniel possess special powers? How was Daniel able to interpret the dream? (verses 25-30)

3. The parts of the statue went from gold to silver to bronze to iron—from the most valuable (gold) to the least valuable (iron). What does that say about the relative quality of the four kingdoms? Will they increase in value or decrease? Does human progress always produce a better society?

Lesson Two

4. The stone that destroyed the statue was "cut out of the mountain without hands;" thus, it was not a human creation. How does its description lead us to believe that it represents Jesus Christ?

_____
_____
_____
_____
_____

You may want to consult with your Bible dictionaries or encyclopedias to learn more about the Aramaic language and the use of furnaces in biblical times. They can be found online here:

Aramaic, https://www.blueletterbible.org/search/Dictionary/viewTopic.cfm?topic=IT0000678

Furnace, https://www.blueletterbible.org/search/Dictionary/viewTopic.cfm?topic=ET0001398

Look over everything that you have discovered so far, and record your most important findings here.

Summarize Your Findings

_____
_____
_____
_____
_____
_____
_____
_____
_____
_____

DANIEL 2:1-49 — 2

You can now put together everything that you have learned and write out your interpretation of this passage. Do not worry that your interpretation may be different from someone else's interpretation. There is more than one way of describing the teachings of this biblical text, and just the activity of putting your thoughts into words will help you to remember the message of Daniel.

Lesson Two

Your Interpretation

In this step, you will record your interpretations of this chapter of Daniel in the areas of Christian beliefs, practices, and spirituality. How does this biblical text inform our beliefs regarding the nature and character of God, the plans and purposes of God, the doctrines of salvation, sanctification, the baptism in the Holy Spirit, sin, healing, the last days, the family, the Church, etc.? Are there issues in this text that you do not understand or that cause you to be uncomfortable? Explain how this text may impact spiritual topics like prayer, fasting, witnessing, testimony, giving, study, worship, sacraments, etc. Write down any interpretations that relate to our beliefs, practices, or spirituality. For example, list the attributes of God that are expressed in verses 20-23. Also, explain the role of prayer in this story.

DANIEL 2:1-49

Devote

In this step of our Bible study, you strengthen your relationship to God. It is not enough to read and study the Bible—we must devote ourselves to serving and worshiping the God of the Bible. It is time to allow the Holy Spirit to speak to you on a deeper level. Basically, you should ask, "God, in light of what You have taught me in Your Word, what do You want me to do?" As you enter into this Devote section, consider the following:

1. By now you have become very familiar with this chapter of Daniel. Therefore, you are ready to let the passage speak to your heart, if you have not already done so. In this step, you should write down the effect this passage has on you as a believer. How does it make you feel? What emotions are brought to the surface as you read the text? Do you feel gratitude, joy, hope, love, heaviness, conviction, guilt, liberty, awe, amazement, or courage?

_____
_____
_____
_____
_____
_____
_____
_____
_____

2. What do you want to do in response to this text? Can you remember a time when you were "put on the spot" like Daniel? Are you facing any situations that call for powerful prayer?

_____
_____
_____

Lesson Two

3. How has this text affected you? Do you sense a transformation of your heart? Do you desire a certain kind of transformation? How is your faith encouraged by Daniel's story?

4. How do you see Proverbs 1:7 reflected in the story of Daniel chapter 2?

DANIEL 2:1-49

Pause for Prayer

At this point, it would be good to pray that the message of Daniel chapter 2 will be realized in your own life. You might want to pray the following:

> Lord, thank You for Your Word that has reawakened in my spirit and life; thank You because You speak and I am changed. You overwhelm me. I ask that You imprint Your image in me. Restore Your likeness in my life. Thank You for Your loving and patient work. Forgive me, Lord, for all my faults and make me pure. Continue to heal me and make me strong and happy in following You. Lord, You are with us, and You are ever drawing us toward You. Draw me, Lord, and I will come, because You have the words of life. I ask also that You help me to bring others to You. Teach me how to be an example to others that I may win them to You. These things we ask in the name of Jesus, our Lord. Amen.

Disciple

The dream of Nebuchadnezzar is a powerful display of God's sovereignty and a bold encouragement for believers. The statue that the king saw in his dream was a manmade object, but the rock was not constructed by human ingenuity or by human energy. The rock, which represents God's kingdom, destroys all human rule and power. Therefore, Daniel's message to God's people is to be strong and to endure until the end when God will establish His ultimate rule on earth. The circumstances that we experience now will be overturned in the end. Despite all present appearances, God will defeat all the forces of sin and evil (see Psalm 73). God's kingdom will expand and fill the earth, just as the rock in the vision became a great mountain. Nebuchadnezzar's dream is an encouragement for the Church to live faithfully in the last days.

God's revelation to Nebuchadnezzar through a dream was considered a normal event within the ancient systems of belief. However, Daniel's ability to tell the dream and to give its interpretation was not normal; it was extraordinary. The Holy Spirit gave Daniel the wisdom necessary to interpret the king's dream. We might ask if God still communicates today through dreams and visions. Unfortunately, many secular people would say, "No." They do not accept the fact that God communicates at all with humans. Moreover, many Christian groups would also say, "No." These Christians are called cessationists, and they believe that the gifts of the Spirit ceased after the death of the apostles. Cessationists believe that God speaks to us only through the Bible, not through the Holy Spirit.

2 Lesson Two

However, as Pentecostals, we accept the truth of Acts 2:17, which declares, "And it shall come to pass in the last days, says God, That I will pour out of My Spirit on all flesh; Your sons and your daughters shall prophesy, Your young men shall see visions, Your old men shall dream dreams" (NKJV). We are living in the last days, and God is continuing to pour out His Spirit upon all flesh. Young people are having visions; old people are dreaming dreams; and God's people are speaking in tongues and prophesying (see 1 Corinthians 12–14). The same Spirit that inspired Daniel is available today to inspire the Spirit-filled church.

One reason that God gives us the gifts and power of the Holy Spirit is to make us better witnesses. Jesus said, "But you will receive power when the Holy Spirit has come upon you; and you shall be My witnesses both in Jerusalem, and in all Judea and Samaria, and even to the remotest part of the earth" (Acts 1:8). In our work of Christian discipleship, we must continually be led and empowered by the Holy Spirit.

The Book of Daniel is a *Path to Faithful Witness*, and Daniel was able to give a faithful witness because the Holy Spirit gave him the wisdom necessary to interpret Nebuchadnezzar's dream. As a faithful witness, you will find opportunities to share the gospel with unbelievers. You will also have occasions to influence other people in their walk with God. This is what discipleship is all about. Write down your commitments that have come forth from studying Daniel 2:1-49. State specific ways that you will bring your life into conformity with teachings of this chapter. I would suggest the following as examples:

This week, I commit to:

1. Being available for God to use me whenever He chooses.

2. Facing every challenge with prayer and with anticipation that the Holy Spirit will give me wisdom.

3. Declaring the Word of God clearly and confidently.

4. Inviting my fellow Christians to join with me in prayer.

5. Maintaining my faithful witness through the power of the Holy Spirit.

ENLIVEN ENCOUNTERING GOD Through HIS WORD

LESSON THREE

DANIEL
3:1-30

FAITHFUL WITNESS UNTO DEATH

Lesson Three

DANIEL 3:1-30 | 3

LESSON THREE

DANIEL 3:1-30

Faithful Witness Unto Death

🗝 KEY VERSE

If it be so, our God whom we serve is able to deliver us from the furnace of blazing fire; and He will deliver us out of your hand, O king. But even if He does not, let it be known to you, O king, that we are not going to serve your gods or worship the golden image that you have set up (Daniel 3:17-18).

Introduction

Let us take a moment to review our progress in the Book of Daniel. In chapter one of Daniel, we are introduced to Daniel and his three friends. They had been captured when the Babylonians invaded Jerusalem. After refusing to defile themselves with the king's meat, they proved to be in better health than all the other young men. Also, the king was impressed with their wisdom and knowledge.

Chapter two of Daniel relates Nebuchadnezzar's dream of a huge statue that symbolized the coming kingdoms. Only Daniel, inspired by God, was able to interpret the king's dream for him. The dream concludes with the overthrow of all human kingdoms and the establishment of God's eternal kingdom. Through his dream, we learn that God directs the course of history to fulfill the divine plan and purpose. Even though we may live in difficult times of great opposition to the Church, we can be assured that God is in control.

In chapter three, the story changes its focus. Instead of Daniel, his three Hebrew friends become the main characters in the narrative. King Nebuchadnezzar, inspired by his dream, builds a huge golden statue and orders everyone to bow down and worship it. Shadrach, Meshach, and Abed-nego, being good Hebrews who worship only Jehovah, refuse to worship the statue; therefore, they are thrown into the fiery furnace for execution. However, God intervenes and delivers them from the fire; whereupon the king declares that "there is no other God who can deliver like this" (Daniel 3:29 NKJV).

3 Lesson Three

Pause for Prayer

Before reading the biblical text, let us pause for prayer, asking God to enlighten our minds and our hearts. Perhaps we could appropriate the prayer of the apostle Paul for the Ephesian believers. Paul prayed:

> Therefore I also, after I heard of your faith in the Lord Jesus and your love for all the saints, do not cease to give thanks for you, making mention of you in my prayers: that the God of our Lord Jesus Christ, the Father of glory, may give to you the spirit of wisdom and revelation in the knowledge of Him, the eyes of your understanding being enlightened; that you may know what is the hope of His calling, what are the riches of the glory of His inheritance in the saints, and what *is* the exceeding greatness of His power toward us who believe, according to the working of His mighty power which He worked in Christ when He raised Him from the dead and seated *Him* at His right hand in the heavenly *places*, far above all principality and power and might and dominion, and every name that is named, not only in this age but also in that which is to come. And He put all *things* under His feet, and gave Him *to be* head over all *things* to the Church, which is His body, the fullness of Him who fills all in all (Ephesians 1:15-23 NKJV).

In the wonderful name of Jesus, we pray. Amen.

The Text

Daniel 3:1-30

¹King Nebuchadnezzar made an image of gold, sixty cubits high and six cubits wide, and set it up on the plain of Dura in the province of Babylon. ² He then summoned the satraps, prefects, governors, advisers, treasurers, judges, magistrates and all the other provincial officials to come to the dedication of the image he had set up. ³ So the satraps, prefects, governors, advisers, treasurers, judges, magistrates

Daniel 3:1-30

and all the other provincial officials assembled for the dedication of the image that King Nebuchadnezzar had set up, and they stood before it.

⁴ Then the herald loudly proclaimed, "Nations and peoples of every language, this is what you are commanded to do: ⁵ As soon as you hear the sound of the horn, flute, zither, lyre, harp, pipe and all kinds of music, you must fall down and worship the image of gold that King Nebuchadnezzar has set up. ⁶ Whoever does not fall down and worship will immediately be thrown into a blazing furnace."

⁷ Therefore, as soon as they heard the sound of the horn, flute, zither, lyre, harp and all kinds of music, all the nations and peoples of every language fell down and worshiped the image of gold that King Nebuchadnezzar had set up.

⁸ At this time some astrologers came forward and denounced the Jews. ⁹ They said to King Nebuchadnezzar, "May the king live forever! ¹⁰ Your Majesty has issued a decree that everyone who hears the sound of the horn, flute, zither, lyre, harp, pipe and all kinds of music must fall down and worship the image of gold, ¹¹ and that whoever does not fall down and worship will be thrown into a blazing furnace. ¹² But there are some Jews whom you have set over the affairs of the province of Babylon—Shadrach, Meshach and Abednego—who pay no attention to you, Your Majesty. They neither serve your gods nor worship the image of gold you have set up."

¹³ Furious with rage, Nebuchadnezzar summoned Shadrach, Meshach and Abednego. So these men were brought before the king, ¹⁴ and Nebuchadnezzar said to them, "Is it true, Shadrach, Meshach and Abednego, that you do not serve my gods or worship the image of gold I have set up? ¹⁵ Now when you hear the sound of the horn, flute, zither, lyre, harp, pipe and all kinds of music, if you are ready to fall

3 Lesson Three

down and worship the image I made, very good. But if you do not worship it, you will be thrown immediately into a blazing furnace. Then what god will be able to rescue you from my hand?"

[16] Shadrach, Meshach and Abednego replied to him, "King Nebuchadnezzar, we do not need to defend ourselves before you in this matter. [17] If we are thrown into the blazing furnace, the God we serve is able to deliver us from it, and he will deliver us from Your Majesty's hand. [18] But even if he does not, we want you to know, Your Majesty, that we will not serve your gods or worship the image of gold you have set up."

[19] Then Nebuchadnezzar was furious with Shadrach, Meshach and Abednego, and his attitude toward them changed. He ordered the furnace heated seven times hotter than usual [20] and commanded some of the strongest soldiers in his army to tie up Shadrach, Meshach and Abednego and throw them into the blazing furnace. [21] So these men, wearing their robes, trousers, turbans and other clothes, were bound and thrown into the blazing furnace. [22] The king's command was so urgent and the furnace so hot that the flames of the fire killed the soldiers who took up Shadrach, Meshach and Abednego, [23] and these three men, firmly tied, fell into the blazing furnace.

[24] Then King Nebuchadnezzar leaped to his feet in amazement and asked his advisers, "Weren't there three men that we tied up and threw into the fire?" They replied, "Certainly, Your Majesty." [25] He said, "Look! I see four men walking around in the fire, unbound and unharmed, and the fourth looks like a son of the gods." [26] Nebuchadnezzar then approached the opening of the blazing furnace and shouted, "Shadrach, Meshach and Abednego, servants of the Most High God, come out! Come here!" So Shadrach, Meshach and Abednego came out of the fire, [27] and the satraps, prefects, governors and royal

DANIEL 3:1-30   3

advisers crowded around them. They saw that the fire had not harmed their bodies, nor was a hair of their heads singed; their robes were not scorched, and there was no smell of fire on them. ²⁸ Then Nebuchadnezzar said, "Praise be to the God of Shadrach, Meshach and Abednego, who has sent his angel and rescued his servants! They trusted in him and defied the king's command and were willing to give up their lives rather than serve or worship any god except their own God. ²⁹ Therefore I decree that the people of any nation or language who say anything against the God of Shadrach, Meshach and Abednego be cut into pieces and their houses be turned into piles of rubble, for no other god can save in this way." ³⁰ Then the king promoted Shadrach, Meshach and Abednego in the province of Babylon.

The Fiery Furnace - A Painting in the Catacombs

DISCOVER

The Discover step is when you dig into the text and learn the Who? What? When? Where? and Why? of the biblical story. It is important that you ask these questions of the text so that you can uncover (that

49

3   Lesson Three

is, "Dis-cover") the important elements in the text. The following Helping Questions will help you to discern the message of Daniel 3:1-30.

Sample Helping Questions

The following questions will help you discover the facts contained in this chapter of Daniel.

1. Reread Daniel 2:49. How does the mention of Daniel's friends lead into Daniel chapter 3?

2. Read chapter 3 of Daniel straight through in order to gain an overall picture of the content and message of the passage. List the main events of this passage.

   Summarize what happens in verses 1-7.

   Summarize what happens in verses 8-12.

50

DANIEL 3:1-30

Summarize what happens in verses 13-18.

Summarize what happens in verses 19-27.

Summarize what happens in verses 28-30.

3. Where was the image of gold located (see v. 1)? Where was Daniel (see Daniel 2:49)?

4. What does Nebuchadnezzar's angry response (vv. 13-15) say about his character?

5. How is God's miraculous deliverance emphasized in verses 26-27?

3 Lesson Three

6. What does Nebuchadnezzar do in response to the miracle of deliverance (verses 28-30)?

Your Helping Questions

DANIEL 3:1-30   3

Your own Helping Questions have discovered many more facts in Daniel 3:1-30. Here are a few more questions that may not have come to mind. Consider these additional questions now.

1. How is Nebuchadnezzar's statue similar but different from the statue in his dream (ch. 2)? What does this say about Nebuchadnezzar?

2. What is the effect of the repetition of lists in verses 2–3 (leaders) and 5-7 (musical instruments)?

3. Compare the endings of chapters 2 and 3. What common messages to you see?

3 Lesson Three

4. Christians are told to respect the government and to obey the law (Romans 13:1). How should we respond to state-sponsored idolatry (see Acts 5:29)?

_____
_____
_____
_____
_____
_____
_____

Pause for Prayer

Before moving on to the Discern step, you should seek for God's wisdom. The Holy Spirit will help you to Discern the meaning of this biblical text. In conclusion to your prayer, you might meditate on the following words that were written in praise to the Word of God:

"How can a young man cleanse his way? By taking heed according to Your word.
With my whole heart I have sought You; oh, let me not wander from Your commandments!

> Your word I have hidden in my heart, that I might not sin against You!
> Blessed are You, O LORD! Teach me Your statutes!
> With my lips I have declared all the judgments of Your mouth.
> I have rejoiced in the way of Your testimonies, as much as in all riches.
> I will meditate on Your precepts, and contemplate Your ways.
> I will delight myself in Your statutes; I will not forget Your word" (Psalm 119:9-16 NKJV).

In Jesus' name, we pray. Amen.

DANIEL 3:1-30   3

DISCERN

Now that you have identified central facts and ideas contained in Daniel chapter 3, you are now prepared to explore the meaning of those facts. The helping tools of the Discern step, with all its symbol marking and marking systems, will bring you closer to producing a well-founded interpretation.

Quickly review all the symbols and highlighting you have employed in the previous lessons of this study guide. Be prepared to reapply these features again in this lesson where appropriate. As always, you can make up some new symbols and highlighting to note special patterns and emphases in Daniel 3:1-30. Select these carefully, because you will want them to work for the rest of your study of Daniel.

→PULLING IT ALL TOGETHER←

You may want to go back and review your answers to the Helping Questions. What important facts have you already discovered? Do you see any patterns or emphases that point to the main message of Daniel 3:1-30? Put together your interpretation and write it below. The following questions may help you to organize your thoughts.

1. Observe the repetition of the words "serve," "servants," and "worship." How many times are they found in Daniel chapter 3? How is that significant?

   _____
   _____
   _____
   _____

2. Observe the repetition of the word "deliver." How many times is "deliver" found in Daniel chapter 3? How is that significant?

   _____
   _____
   _____

Lesson Three

3. Take note of the repetition of the words "God," "god," and "gods." How does the repeated use of these terms add to the meaning of this chapter?

4. Compare Daniel chapter 3 to Psalm 91 and write down your comparison.

5. Did the three Hebrews believe that God *could* deliver them? Did they believe that God *would* deliver them? Why did they not compromise?

You may want to consult with your Bible dictionaries or encyclopedias to learn the length of a "cubit" (3:1) and the meaning of the word "satrap" (3:2). You may also want to identify the musical instrument called the "trigon" (3:5). These subjects can be found online here:

Cubit, https://www.blueletterbible.org/search/Dictionary/viewTopic.cfm?topic=ET0000934

Satraps, translated "princes" in the KJV, https://www.merriam-webster.com/dictionary/satrap

The trigon, translated "sackbut" in the KJV, is described here:
　　　　https://www.blueletterbible.org/search/Dictionary/viewTopic.cfm?topic=ET0003177

Daniel 3:1-30

Summarize your findings by writing down some of the most important points that have arisen in your study of Daniel chapter 3.

Summarize Your Findings

Lesson Three

Your Interpretation

In this step, you will record your interpretations of this chapter of Daniel in the areas of Christian beliefs, practices, and spirituality. How does this biblical text inform our beliefs regarding the nature and character of God, the plans and purposes of God, the doctrines of salvation, sanctification, the baptism in the Holy Spirit, sin, healing, the last days, the family, the Church, etc.? Are there issues in this text that you do not understand or that cause you to be uncomfortable? Explain how this text may impact spiritual topics like prayer, fasting, witnessing, testimony, giving, study, worship, sacraments, etc. Write down any interpretations that relate to our beliefs, practices, or spirituality. For example, what might lead you to believe that the fourth person in the fire is the preincarnate Jesus? What might suggest that the person was an angel?

DANIEL 3:1-30 | 3

Devote

In this step of our Bible study, you strengthen your relationship to God. It is not enough to read and study the Bible—we must devote ourselves to serving and worshiping the God of the Bible. It is time to allow the Holy Spirit to speak to you on a deeper level. Basically, you should ask, "God, in light of what You have taught me in Your Word, what do You want me to do?" As you enter into this Devote section, consider the following:

How does the statement of the three Hebrews correspond to your own belief in God's power to deliver (see verses 16-18)? How are we temped to compromise? What are the false gods that people worship today?

_____
_____
_____
_____
_____

1. By now you have become very familiar with this chapter of Daniel. Therefore, you are ready to let the passage speak to your heart, if you have not already done so. In this step, you should write down the effect this passage has on you as a believer. How does it make you feel? What emotions are brought to the surface as you read the text? Do you feel gratitude, joy, hope, love, heaviness, conviction, guilt, liberty, awe, amazement, or courage?

_____
_____
_____
_____
_____
_____

Lesson Three

2. What do you want to do in response to this text? What beliefs do you hold that you cannot compromise? What convictions would you die for?

_____
_____
_____
_____

3. How is our culture putting pressure on you to compromise your beliefs? How does this biblical text help you to meet these challenges? Do you sense a transformation of your heart? Do you desire a certain kind of transformation?

_____
_____
_____
_____
_____

Pause for Prayer

You should pause once again for prayer, asking God to reveal to you His perfect will. Ask Him to show you how the message of Daniel can be fully realized in your life. You may find inspiration in the following prayer that was prayed by Saint Anselm of Canterbury:

> Teach me to seek you, and reveal yourself to me as I seek: For unless you instruct me I cannot seek you, and unless you reveal yourself I cannot find you. Let me seek you in desiring you: let me desire you in seeking you. Let me find you in loving you: let me love you in finding you.

In the wonderful name of Jesus, we pray. Amen.

DANIEL 3:1-30 | 3

⳨ DISCIPLE

As you come to the close of your third lesson, you have begun to see how the Book of Daniel is a *Path to Faithful Witness*. The three Hebrews (Shadrach, Meshach, and Abed-nego) were ready to give a faithful witness even unto death. Their faithfulness reminds me of the following Scripture: "Do not fear what you are about to suffer. Behold, the devil is about to cast some of you into prison, that you may be tested, and you will have tribulation ten days. Be faithful until death, and I will give you the crown of life" (Revelation 2:10).

As a faithful witness, you will find opportunities to share the gospel with unbelievers. You will also have occasions to influence other people in their walk with God. This is what discipleship is all about. Write down your commitments that have come forth from studying Daniel 3:1-30. State specific ways that you will bring your life into conformity with teachings of this chapter. I would suggest the following as examples:

This week, I commit to:

1. Being a good citizen and showing my support for the beneficial policies of my government.
2. Praying daily for the leaders of my city, my state, and my nation.
3. Honoring the law of God above all human laws.
4. Resisting any and all compromises in regard to idolatry.
5. Maintaining my faithful witness of Jesus, even if my witness leads to death.

THE FIERY FURNACE—BY HEURES D'HENRI II

ENLIVEN
ENCOUNTERING GOD
Through
HIS WORD

LESSON FOUR

DANIEL
4:1-37

FAITHFUL WITNESS
OF GOD'S SOVEREIGNTY

4 Lesson Four

DANIEL 4:1-37

LESSON FOUR

DANIEL 4:1-37

Faithful Witness of God's Sovereignty

KEY VERSE

This sentence is by the decree of the angelic watchers, and the decision is a command of the holy ones, in order that the living may know that the Most High is ruler over the realm of mankind, and bestows it on whom He wishes, and sets over it the lowliest of men (Daniel 4:17).

Introduction

It would seem that Nebuchadnezzar, having witnessed the dramatic revelations given to Daniel and the miraculous deliverance of Shadrach, Meshach, and Abed-nego, would have acquired a sober attitude and a bit of humility. Humility, however, was not a common trait among ancient monarchs. In Daniel's time, the kings ruled with an iron fist. Their authority and their decisions were not to be questioned. In fact, in the ancient Near Eastern worldview, kings were often considered divine beings who should be worshiped. Nebuchadnezzar, however, would learn that he was far from divine. In fact, he would soon be brought down to the level of an animal.

Although none of us are likely to be in a position like Nebuchadnezzar, we are, nevertheless, tempted to exalt ourselves in pride. We would do well to remember that all our good works, all our talents, all our possessions, and all our accomplishments are gifts from God (1 Corinthians 1:26-29; 3:6-7; 15:10).

4 Lesson Four

Pause for Prayer

Before you read Daniel 4:1-37, you should pray for the wisdom that comes only from God. Pray for insight and illumination. Pray for a joyous time of study. At the beginning of your prayer, consider this prayer of Saint Augustine, who prayed,

> Let your Scriptures be my pure delight… O Lord, perfect me and reveal those pages to me! See, your voice is my joy. Give me what I love… May the inner secrets of your words be laid open to me when I knock. This I beg by our Lord Jesus Christ in whom are hidden all the treasures of wisdom and knowledge (Colossians 2:3). These are the treasures I seek in your books.

In the wonderful name of Jesus, we pray. Amen.

The Text

Daniel 4:1-37

¹King Nebuchadnezzar, to the nations and peoples of every language, who live in all the earth: May you prosper greatly! ²It is my pleasure to tell you about the miraculous signs and wonders that the Most High God has performed for me. ³How great are his signs, how mighty his wonders! His kingdom is an eternal kingdom; his dominion endures from generation to generation.

⁴I, Nebuchadnezzar, was at home in my palace, contented and prosperous. ⁵I had a dream that made me afraid. As I was lying in bed, the images and visions that passed through my mind terrified me. ⁶So I commanded that all the wise men of Babylon be brought before me to interpret the dream for me. ⁷When the magicians, enchanters, astrologers and diviners came, I told them the dream, but they

DANIEL 4:1-37   4

could not interpret it for me. ⁸ Finally, Daniel came into my presence and I told him the dream. (He is called Belteshazzar, after the name of my god, and the spirit of the holy gods is in him.)

⁹ I said, "Belteshazzar, chief of the magicians, I know that the spirit of the holy gods is in you, and no mystery is too difficult for you. Here is my dream; interpret it for me. ¹⁰ These are the visions I saw while lying in bed: I looked, and there before me stood a tree in the middle of the land. Its height was enormous. ¹¹ The tree grew large and strong and its top touched the sky; it was visible to the ends of the earth. ¹² Its leaves were beautiful, its fruit abundant, and on it was food for all. Under it the wild animals found shelter, and the birds lived in its branches; from it every creature was fed. ¹³ "In the visions I saw while lying in bed, I looked, and there before me was a holy one, a messenger, coming down from heaven. ¹⁴ He called in a loud voice: 'Cut down the tree and trim off its branches; strip off its leaves and scatter its fruit. Let the animals flee from under it and the birds from its branches. ¹⁵ But let the stump and its roots, bound with iron and bronze, remain in the ground, in the grass of the field. "'Let him be drenched with the dew of heaven, and let him live with the animals among the plants of the earth. ¹⁶ Let his mind be changed from that of a man and let him be given the mind of an animal, till seven times pass by for him. ¹⁷ "'The decision is announced by messengers, the holy ones declare the verdict, so that the living may know that the Most High is sovereign over

Nebuchadnezzar Dreams of a Great Tree
Illustration in a Medieval Bible

67

4 Lesson Four

all kingdoms on earth and gives them to anyone he wishes and sets over them the lowliest of people.'

¹⁸ "This is the dream that I, King Nebuchadnezzar, had. Now, Belteshazzar, tell me what it means, for none of the wise men in my kingdom can interpret it for me. But you can, because the spirit of the holy gods is in you."

¹⁹ Then Daniel (also called Belteshazzar) was greatly perplexed for a time, and his thoughts terrified him. So the king said, "Belteshazzar, do not let the dream or its meaning alarm you." Belteshazzar answered, "My lord, if only the dream applied to your enemies and its meaning to your adversaries! ²⁰ The tree you saw, which grew large and strong, with its top touching the sky, visible to the whole earth, ²¹ with beautiful leaves and abundant fruit, providing food for all, giving shelter to the wild animals, and having nesting places in its branches for the birds— ²² Your Majesty, you are that tree! You have become great and strong; your greatness has grown until it reaches the sky, and your dominion extends to distant parts of the earth.

²³ "Your Majesty saw a holy one, a messenger, coming down from heaven and saying, 'Cut down the tree and destroy it, but leave the stump, bound with iron and bronze, in the grass of the field, while its roots remain in the ground. Let him be drenched with the dew of heaven; let him live with the wild animals, until seven times pass by for him.' ²⁴ "This is the interpretation, Your Majesty, and this is the decree the Most High has issued against my lord the king: ²⁵ You will be driven away from people and will live with the wild animals; you will eat grass like the ox and be drenched with the dew of heaven. Seven times will pass by for you until you acknowledge that the Most High is sovereign over all kingdoms on earth and gives them to anyone he wishes. ²⁶ The command to leave the stump of the tree with its roots means that your kingdom will be restored to you when you acknowledge that Heaven

rules. ²⁷ Therefore, Your Majesty, be pleased to accept my advice: Renounce your sins by doing what is right, and your wickedness by being kind to the oppressed. It may be that then your prosperity will continue." ²⁸ All this happened to King Nebuchadnezzar. ²⁹ Twelve months later, as the king was walking on the roof of the royal palace of Babylon, ³⁰ he said, "Is not this the great Babylon I have built as the royal residence, by my mighty power and for the glory of my majesty?" ³¹ Even as the words were on his lips, a voice came from heaven, "This is what is decreed for you, King Nebuchadnezzar: Your royal authority has been taken from you. ³² You will be driven away from people and will live with the wild animals; you will eat grass like the ox. Seven times will pass by for you until you acknowledge that the Most High is sovereign over all kingdoms on earth and gives them to anyone he wishes." ³³ Immediately what had been said about Nebuchadnezzar was fulfilled. He was driven away from people and ate grass like the ox. His body was drenched with the dew of heaven until his hair grew like the feathers of an eagle and his nails like the claws of a bird.

³⁴ At the end of that time, I, Nebuchadnezzar, raised my eyes toward heaven, and my sanity was restored. Then I praised the Most High; I honored and glorified him who lives forever. His dominion is an eternal dominion; his kingdom endures from generation to generation. ³⁵ All the peoples of the earth are regarded as nothing. He does as he pleases with the powers of heaven and the peoples of the earth. No one can hold back his hand or say to him: "What have you done?" ³⁶ At the same time that my sanity was restored, my honor and splendor were returned to me for the glory of my kingdom. My advisers and nobles sought me out, and I was restored to my throne and became even greater than before. ³⁷ Now I, Nebuchadnezzar, praise and exalt and glorify the King of heaven, because everything he does is right and all his ways are just. And those who walk in pride he is able to humble.

4 Lesson Four

Discover

This chapter of the Book of Daniel is filled with powerful lessons for today's Christian. As you read and study the biblical text, allow the Holy Spirit to speak to you and apply the Scripture to your own life. The following Helping Questions will guide you to Discover many of the truths contained in this chapter of Daniel.

Sample Helping Questions

1. Read chapter 4 of Daniel straight through in order to gain an overall picture of the content and message of the passage. List the main events of this passage.

   What happens in verses 1-3?

   _____
   _____
   _____

   What happens in verses 4-18?

   _____
   _____
   _____

   What happens in verses 19-27?

   _____
   _____
   _____

   What happens in verses 28-33?

   _____
   _____
   _____

DANIEL 4:1-37   4

What happens in verses 34-37?

If you put together your descriptions above, you will have an outline of chapter 4.

2. Who is the speaker in Daniel 4:1, 4:4, and 4:34? Why do you suppose that the speaker here is different from the speaker in chapters 1–3?

3. Why do you suppose Nebuchadnezzar began his story with praise to God? How does he end the story in verse 37?

4. In chapter 1, Daniel proved that he and his friends were the best of all the young men who had been chosen to serve the king. In chapter 2, Daniel interpreted Nebuchadnezzar's vision of the statue made of gold, silver, bronze, iron, and clay. Now, the king calls upon Daniel again. How does the king express his confidence in Daniel here in verses 8, 9, and 18?

Lesson Four

5. Nebuchadnezzar is a polytheist—one who believes in many gods—and he does not fully comprehend the God of Israel. Nevertheless, he is aware that Daniel is different from all the other wise men. According to the king, what makes Daniel different from the other advisors?

_____

_____

_____

_____

6. Why did Nebuchadnezzar address Daniel as "Belteshazzar"? How do you think Daniel felt when the king spoke to him using his Babylonian name?

_____

_____

_____

_____

_____

In each encounter with the king, Daniel proclaimed that his wisdom and abilities came from God. Therefore, the king is now convinced that "a spirit of the holy gods is in" Daniel. Because he has the Spirit in him, Daniel is not troubled by any secret. That is, when faced with a mystery, he does not get upset, distressed, or worried. His trust is in the Lord, who is able to reveal all mysteries (see Daniel 2:28).

Daniel immediately knows the meaning of the dream, but he hesitates to speak it. The seriousness of the interpretation causes him to be stunned for a short time. The word "appalled" means that Daniel was shocked, or stunned. We learned earlier that no mystery could "trouble" Daniel, but now we read that the interpretation "troubled" him. However, Daniel is not troubled by the difficulty of the mystery; he is troubled by the implications of its meaning. He is troubled, because he knows that the king will not be pleased when he hears the interpretation. Therefore, Daniel is distressed by the impact the interpretation will have upon Nebuchadnezzar.

DANIEL 4:1-37   **4**

The king, however, encourages Daniel; and once Daniel collects his thoughts, he speaks to the king. He prefaces his remarks with the wish that the dream's bad news might be applied to the king's enemies. In effect, Daniel says, "I wish the dream would happen to those who hate you, and I wish its meaning would go against your enemies instead of against you." Nevertheless, Daniel knows that the dream is aimed directly at King Nebuchadnezzar.

Take time to develop some of your own Helping Questions to bring the central facts of this passage to light. Think carefully about the kind of questions that you bring to the Bible. Just thinking in this way "draws you into" ("inductive") the wisdom of God's Word. So, make up some questions and do your best to provide answers that uncover the great truths of the Bible.

Your Helping Questions

Lesson Four

Your own Helping Questions have uncovered many more facts in Daniel 4:1-7. Here are a few more questions that may not have come to mind. Consider these additional questions now.

1. The "watcher" who descends from heaven is a supernatural being, sent as a messenger of God. The watcher is also called "a holy one," and both terms are used by the Jews to describe the angels of God. The Book of Enoch several times refers to the angels as "watchers" and "holy ones," as does also the Book of Jubilees and the Dead Sea Scroll called the Genesis Apocryphon (These Jewish books were written in the Intertestamental Period, but they are not considered to be Scripture). Why do you suppose that these particular angels are called "watchers"? (see, for example, Zechariah 1:9-11.)

2. Prophetic messages often allowed room for the hearer to repent. The best example is the city of Nineveh, which repented because of the preaching of Jonah. Their repentance caused God to change His mind and not destroy the city. Does Daniel believe that the fulfilment of the king's dream is conditional? Can the outcome be changed if the king repents? Explain.

DANIEL 4:1-37

3. Daniel advises Nebuchadnezzar to repent of his sins in hopes that God would change His judgment. However, Daniel counsels the king to do more than just confess his guilt; he must make specific changes. What are the changes that Daniel calls for?

4. God gives Nebuchadnezzar plenty of time to repent and to change his ways. What happened after one year had passed? Had the king made the required changes in his life? Had his pride and arrogance decreased?

5. The phrase "seven periods of time" is ambiguous and open-ended. Do you think it refers to seven days, seven months, or seven years? Explain your reasons.

4 Lesson Four

Discern

As soon as Nebuchadnezzar declares that he had built Babylon by his own power and for his own glory, he is instantly turned into an animal, and he is driven into the wilderness. Historians tell us that the ancient city of Babylon was a marvelous accomplishment, with impenetrable walls and magnificent buildings. One of the Seven Wonders of the Ancient World was the awe-inspiring Hanging Gardens of Babylon. However, the king had not built Babylon by his own power and ingenuity. Daniel had already explained clearly to the king that it is God who gives the power to human rulers. It is God who grants authority for the building of empires. No doubt, Nebuchadnezzar was surrounded by advisors and friends who praised him without ceasing. Therefore, the king ignored Daniel's teachings about the sovereignty of God.

Before the king's proud words are out of his mouth, he heard a voice from heaven speaking to him and saying, "The kingdom has departed from you" (verse 31 NKJV). The voice continued to repeat the interpretation of the dream that Daniel had given to the king twelve months earlier. The king would be with the animals in the field, and he would eat grass like an ox until "seven times" pass over him and he learns that the Most High God rules over all of humanity and gives authority to whomever He wills (verse 32).

The Discern step will prove very helpful in interpreting this chapter of the Book of Daniel. All of the symbols and markings that you have developed up to this point will be put to good use in interpreting this passage. These markings can go a long way to help you visualize the important points in this section of Scripture. However, as always, we need the Spirit of Truth to guide us in our study. Therefore, let us pray for God's guidance as we Discern the meaning of Daniel chapter 4.

Pause for Prayer

At the conclusion of your prayer, meditate upon the following Scripture passage in which the psalmist seeks for deeper understanding of God's Word:

> My soul clings to the dust; revive me according to Your word.
>
> I have declared my ways, and You answered me; teach me Your statutes.
>
> Make me understand the way of Your precepts; so shall I meditate on Your wondrous works.

[handwritten: a guide respecting moral conduct.]

DANIEL 4:1-37

4

My soul melts from heaviness; strengthen me according to Your word.

Remove from me the way of lying, and grant me Your law graciously.

I have chosen the way of truth; Your judgments I have laid before me.

I cling to Your testimonies; O LORD, do not put me to shame!

I will run the course of Your commandments, for You shall enlarge my heart

(Psalm 119:25-32 NKJV).

In the wonderful name of Jesus, we pray. Amen.

NEBUCHADNEZZAR REGAINS HIS SANITY—BY JACOB SYMONSZ PYNAS

Review the helping tools that you used in previous lessons. You can see how some of the symbols and highlighting can be applied to this chapter of Daniel. Be ready to create new symbols or markings when the occasion calls for it. Be creative and read carefully. Remember that the more vivid the helping tool, the more it will communicate what is in the Bible. Also, the more vivid the marking system, the easier it will be for you to remember the ideas that are represented. Always employ symbols that have worked for you in past lessons. This will reinforce the power of the marking system to convey a particular aspect of the text.

77

4 Lesson Four

→Pulling It All Together←

1. Everything was going extremely well for Nebuchadnezzar, the king of Babylon. He was "at ease" and "flourishing" in his royal palace (verse 4). He enjoyed a life of luxury and ease, surrounded by servants who obeyed his every wish and by guards who protected him from any and all dangers. Why would he be disturbed by this dream?

   _____
   _____
   _____
   _____

2. Daniel explains that the dream is a prophetic warning in the form of an allegory. The king saw a tree that was strong and tall. Its influence reached throughout the earth. The use of a tree as a symbol for the king is found in the literature of Mesopotamia and in other parts of Scripture (Isaiah 2:12-13; 10:34; Ezekiel 17 and 31). How was Nebuchadnezzar like the tree in his dream?

   _____
   _____
   _____
   _____

3. Explain why God judged Nebuchadnezzar.

   _____
   _____
   _____
   _____

DANIEL 4:1-37

4. Other evil rulers were given no opportunity to repent (see, for example, Daniel 5:30 and Acts 12:21-23). Why do you think that God offered grace to Nebuchadnezzar?

5. List the attributes and qualities of God that Nebuchadnezzar states in verses 34-37.

6. How many times is God called "the Most High"? What does Nebuchadnezzar's use of that term say about his view of God? Is God the "Most High" in your life? In your church?

4 Lesson Four

7. How many times are the words "kingdom" and "dominion" used in this chapter of Daniel? What does the repeated use of these terms say about the message of the chapter?

Review all the work that you have done on Daniel chapter 4. Summarize the main points in the space provided below. Be mindful that this summary will greatly inform your interpretation.

Summarize Your Findings

DANIEL 4:1-37

Your Interpretation

All kinds of information have come forth by way of the Helping Questions and the helping tools. At this point, review everything carefully and jot down some notes. Now is the time to engage everything that you have learned thus far and answer the all-important question: What does this passage mean? How does this biblical text inform our beliefs regarding the nature and character of God, the plans and purposes of God, the doctrines of salvation, sanctification, Holy Spirit, sin, healing, the last days, the family, the Church, etc.? Are there issues in this text that you do not understand or that cause you to be uncomfortable? Explain how this text may impact spiritual topics like prayer, fasting, witnessing, testimony, giving, study, worship, sacraments, etc. Write down any interpretations that relate to our beliefs, practices, or spirituality.

Lesson Four

You may want to consult with your Bible dictionaries or encyclopedias to learn more about the "watchers." The definition of "watcher" can be found online here:

Watcher, https://www.blueletterbible.org/search/Dictionary/viewTopic.cfm?topic=IT0009136

Devote

In this step of our Bible study, you strengthen your relationship to God. It is not enough to read and study the Bible—we must devote ourselves to serving and worshiping the God of the Bible. It is time to allow the Holy Spirit to speak to you on a deeper level. Basically, you should ask, "God, in light of what you have taught me in your Word, what do you want me to do?"

We must not overlook the parallels between the king's dream and the story of the Tower of Babel, the story from which Babylon gets its name (Genesis 11). The people in Genesis built a city and a tower, and the tower was meant to "reach unto heaven" (Genesis 11:4). Their goal was to make for themselves "a name." Thus, their motivation for building came from their pride and arrogance. As a judgment on their pride, God came down and confused their language and scattered them over the face of the earth.

Nebuchadnezzar is king of Babylon many centuries later, but his ambitions are no less than those of his ancestors. In fact, he has gone beyond them in his accomplishments. He built not only a city and a tower but also an empire. His greatness reached up to heaven, which may suggest that he thought of himself as a god. Certainly, he had made for himself "a name." Just as God judged the builders of the Tower of Babel and as God judged Nebuchadnezzar, He will also judge us if we have pride in our hearts.

As you enter into this Devote section, consider the following:

1. By now you have become very familiar with this chapter of Daniel. Therefore, you are ready to let the passage speak to your heart, if you have not already done so. In this step, you should write down the effect this passage has on you as a believer. How does it make you feel? What emotions are brought to the surface as you read the text? Do you feel gratitude, joy, hope, love, heaviness, conviction, guilt, liberty, awe, amazement, or courage?

_____

_____

_____

_____

DANIEL 4:1-37 | 4

2. Do you harbor feelings of pride and arrogance? Read 1 Corinthians 1:26-31. What do you want to do in response to this text?

_____

_____

_____

_____

_____

3. How has this text affected you? Do you sense a transformation of your heart? Do you desire a certain kind of transformation? See Luke 1:52; James 4:6; and 1 Peter 5:5-6.

_____

_____

_____

_____

_____

_____

_____

_____

PAUSE *for* PRAYER

Our Father in heaven, thank You for the Holy Spirit that is guiding and teaching me to know Your will. Lord of heaven, thank You because You have enabled me to keep on trusting You. Your Word is life and Spirit to me. May it help me to know and trust You more. Thank You for sending the Word to heal and to deliver us from destruction. As I meditate on it, may it remain in my heart so that it can strengthen me at the appointed time. Thank You, Lord, because You have never failed me; You always keep Your Word and are looking at it to make sure it accomplishes what it was sent to do. Thank You for hearing and answering my prayer. In the wonderful name of Jesus, I pray. Amen.

Lesson Four

✞ ⟨≻ DISCIPLE

As you come to the close of your fourth lesson, you have begun to see how the Book of Daniel is a *Path to Faithful Witness*. In chapter 4 of the Book of Daniel, both Daniel and Nebuchadnezzar serve as witnesses to God's sovereignty over the events of the world. In the midst of his prosperity, Nebuchadnezzar dreamed a dream that disturbed him greatly. The Babylonians, like everyone else in the ancient Near East, believed that dreams were important indicators of one's character and one's destiny. This dream was different, however, because it was inspired by the Lord. The dream was God's way of speaking to the powerful king through a means that he would receive. God speaks in many different ways, and He knows how to communicate with each individual. Even today, God speaks through preaching, teaching, music, testimonies, Scripture, dreams, visions, art, and the gifts of the Spirit.

The story of Nebuchadnezzar's humiliation reminds us of the wise proverb, "Pride goes before destruction, And a haughty spirit before a fall" (Proverbs 16:18 NKJV). The proverb was probably in Paul's mind when he wrote to the Corinthian church the following exhortation: "Therefore let him who thinks he stands take heed lest he fall. No temptation has overtaken you except such as is common to man; but God is faithful, who will not allow you to be tempted beyond what you are able, but with the temptation will also make the way of escape, that you may be able to bear it" (1 Corinthians 10:12-13 NKJV). We should notice that "falling" is not inevitable, because God will make a way of escape for whoever is tempted. We remember that even Nebuchadnezzar was given a warning by Daniel that included a 12-month grace period. However, the king did not take advantage of the grace that was offered to him. Therefore, God had no option but to follow through with punishment. Further evidence of God's grace may be seen in His restoration of King Nebuchadnezzar, who was given a second chance for change. Let us be careful to take advantage of the "way of escape" that God offers to us.

The tree in Nebuchadnezzar's dream symbolized the divine world order that was maintained by the king who represented that order which was established by God. As king, Nebuchadnezzar's power and authority carried with it great responsibility. As Christians, our many blessings also come with great responsibilities. We must be faithful witnesses for Jesus Christ as we live out the gospel every day. The Church is God's visible presence on the earth, and we must represent Jesus as good ambassadors who lead people to be reconciled to God. Discipleship is our responsibility.

At this point, you should write down your commitments that result from your study of Daniel 4:1-37. State specific ways that you will bring your life into conformity with teachings of this chapter. I would suggest the following as examples:

This week, I commit to:

1. Acknowledging the sovereignty of God over every aspect of my life.
2. Seeking out ways that I can be a faithful witness.
3. Humbling myself before God, recognizing my weaknesses, my flaws, and my failures.
4. Praying for my Church, that it will be a light in the darkness.

ENLIVEN ENCOUNTERING GOD Through HIS WORD

LESSON FIVE

DANIEL
5:1-31

FAITHFUL WITNESS OF GOD'S JUDGMENT

Lesson Five

Lesson Five

Daniel 5:1-31

Faithful Witness of God's Judgment

Key Verse

But you have exalted yourself against the Lord of heaven; and they have brought the vessels of His house before you, and you and your nobles, your wives and your concubines have been drinking wine from them; and you have praised the gods of silver and gold, of bronze, iron, wood and stone, which do not see, hear or understand. But the God in whose hand are your life-breath and your ways, you have not glorified (Daniel 5:23).

Introduction

When the fifth chapter of Daniel opens, there is a new king on the throne of Babylon. Nothing is said about the death of Nebuchadnezzar, or how Belshazzar, a descendant of Nebuchadnezzar, came to sit on the throne. In fact, nothing is said about Belshazzar's rule except for one fateful evening, which would be his last evening on earth.

We learn in Daniel 5 that Belshazzar profaned the vessels that had been stolen from God's Temple in Jerusalem. He used the vessels during his drunken party as he praised his pagan idols. In the midst of his great feast, Belshazzar saw a vision of a hand that wrote on the wall a message of God's judgment. Daniel was brought in to interpret the miraculous writing, and he had the opportunity to serve as a "Faithful Witness of God's Judgment." Unlike Nebuchadnezzar (in chapter 4), King Belshazzar was not granted a grace-period. Apparently, his heart was so hardened he was beyond redemption; therefore, he perished just at the time he was desecrating and profaning the sacred vessels. God's judgment of Belshazzar is a warning to people everywhere, including Christians, that the sacred things of God must be honored.

Lesson Five

Pause for Prayer

Take a moment and pray that the Holy Spirit will make known to you the will of God as revealed in Daniel chapter 5. After your prayer, think about the following Scripture in which the psalmist prays for understanding:

Teach me, O Lord, the way of Your statutes, and I shall keep it to the end.

Give me understanding, and I shall keep Your law; indeed, I shall observe it with my whole heart.

Make me walk in the path of Your commandments, for I delight in it.

Incline my heart to Your testimonies, and not to covetousness.

Turn away my eyes from looking at worthless things, and revive me in Your way.

Establish Your word to Your servant, who is devoted to fearing You.

Turn away my reproach which I dread, for Your judgments are good.

Behold, I long for Your precepts; revive me in Your righteousness (Psalm 119:33-40 NKJV).

The Text

Daniel 5:1-31

¹King Belshazzar gave a great banquet for a thousand of his nobles and drank wine with them. ²While Belshazzar was drinking his wine, he gave orders to bring in the gold and silver goblets that Nebuchadnezzar his father had taken from the temple in Jerusalem, so that the king and his nobles, his wives and his concubines might drink from them. ³So they brought in the gold goblets that had been taken from the temple of God in Jerusalem, and the king and his nobles, his wives and his concubines drank from them. ⁴As they drank the wine, they praised the gods of gold and silver, of bronze, iron, wood and stone.

DANIEL 5:1-31

⁵ Suddenly the fingers of a human hand appeared and wrote on the plaster of the wall, near the lampstand in the royal palace. The king watched the hand as it wrote. ⁶ His face turned pale and he was so frightened that his legs became weak and his knees were knocking.

⁷ The king summoned the enchanters, astrologers and diviners. Then he said to these wise men of Babylon, "Whoever reads this writing and tells me what it means will be clothed in purple and have a gold chain placed around his neck, and he will be made the third highest ruler in the kingdom."

⁸ Then all the king's wise men came in, but they could not read the writing or tell the king what it meant. ⁹ So King Belshazzar became even more terrified and his face grew more pale. His nobles were baffled.

¹⁰ The queen, hearing the voices of the king and his nobles, came into the banquet hall. "May the king live forever!" she said. "Don't be alarmed! Don't look so pale! ¹¹ There is a man in your kingdom who has the spirit of the holy gods in him. In the time of your father he was found to have insight and intelligence and wisdom like that of the gods. Your father, King Nebuchadnezzar, appointed him chief of the magicians, enchanters, astrologers and diviners. ¹² He did this because Daniel, whom the king called Belteshazzar, was found to have a keen mind and knowledge and understanding, and also the ability to interpret dreams, explain riddles and solve difficult problems. Call for Daniel, and he will tell you what the writing means."

¹³ So Daniel was brought before the king, and the king said to him, "Are you Daniel, one of the exiles my father the king brought from Judah? ¹⁴ I have heard that the spirit of the gods is in you and that you have insight, intelligence and outstanding wisdom. ¹⁵ The wise men and enchanters were brought before me to read this writing and tell me what it means, but they could not explain it. ¹⁶ Now I have heard that

5 Lesson Five

you are able to give interpretations and to solve difficult problems. If you can read this writing and tell me what it means, you will be clothed in purple and have a gold chain placed around your neck, and you will be made the third highest ruler in the kingdom."

[17] Then Daniel answered the king, "You may keep your gifts for yourself and give your rewards to someone else. Nevertheless, I will read the writing for the king and tell him what it means.

[18] "Your Majesty, the Most High God gave your father Nebuchadnezzar sovereignty and greatness and glory and splendor. [19] Because of the high position he gave him, all the nations and peoples of every language dreaded and feared him. Those the king wanted to put to death, he put to death; those he wanted to spare, he spared; those he wanted to promote, he promoted; and those he wanted to humble, he humbled. [20] But when his heart became arrogant and hardened with pride, he was deposed from his royal throne and stripped of his glory. [21] He was driven away from people and given the mind of an animal; he lived with the wild donkeys and ate grass like the ox; and his body was drenched with the dew of heaven, until he acknowledged that the Most High God is sovereign over all kingdoms on earth and sets over them anyone he wishes. [22] "But you, Belshazzar, his son, have not humbled yourself, though you knew all this. [23] Instead, you have set yourself up against the Lord of heaven. You had the goblets from his temple brought to you, and you and your nobles, your wives and your concubines drank wine from them. You praised the gods of silver and gold, of bronze, iron, wood and stone, which cannot see or hear or understand. But you did not honor the God who holds in his hand your life and all your ways. [24] Therefore he sent the hand that wrote the inscription.

[25] "This is the inscription that was written: mene, mene, tekel, parsin. [26] "Here is what these words mean:

Mene—God has numbered the days of your reign and brought it to an end.

DANIEL 5:1-31

²⁷ *Tekel*—You have been weighed on the scales and found wanting.

²⁸ *Peres*—Your kingdom is divided and given to the Medes and Persians."

²⁹ Then at Belshazzar's command, Daniel was clothed in purple, a gold chain was placed around his neck, and he was proclaimed the third highest ruler in the kingdom.

³⁰ That very night Belshazzar, king of the Babylonians, was slain, ³¹ and Darius the Mede took over the kingdom, at the age of sixty-two.

BELSHAZZAR SEES THE HANDWRITING ON THE WALL—BY REMBRANDT

93

5   Lesson Five

Discover

Perhaps a little background information would be helpful at this point. Daniel 5 leaps from the reign of Nebuchadnezzar and the glory days of Babylon to the decline of Babylon and the rule of Belshazzar. Nebuchadnezzar is referred to as Belshazzar's "father" (Daniel 5:2, 11, 13, 18), but the word "father" often means "ancestor," as it does here. During the events of the first four chapters of Daniel, the king of Babylon is Nebuchadnezzar. He ruled for 43 years and died in 562 BC. After his death, the kingdom was ruled by a series of kings whose reigns were brief and tumultuous. Nebuchadnezzar's son Evil-Merodach ruled for two years (2 Kings 25:27-30) before he was murdered by his brother-in-law Neriglissar (also called Nergal-Sharezer). Neriglissar reigned four years (Jeremiah 39:3, 13) before he died. After him came his young son Labashi-Marduk, who ruled only two months before he was assassinated by Nabonidus, who reigned 17 years. Nabonidus attempted to restore the glory of Babylon and to expand the religion of Babylon. After conquering parts of Arabia, he decided to live there during the last days of his reign. At the same time, Nabonidus appointed his son Belshazzar to rule in Babylon in his absence. The name "Belshazzar" is similar to but not exactly the same as "Belteshazzar," which was Daniel's Babylonian name. Belteshazzar means "may Bel protect his life," but Belshazzar means "O Bel, protect the king."

The Babylonian Empire was under attack by the Persians, but Belshazzar would not have been afraid. The walls around Babylon were considered impenetrable, and the city had supplies of food enough to last for 20 years. Having little concern about the city's safety, Belshazzar throws a massive party, a feast for 1000 people. Archaeologists have discovered the remains of a large banquet hall that measured 165 feet long and 55 feet wide, which would have been large enough to hold 1000 guests, especially if it had a balcony. Belshazzar's feast would be the equivalent of what we might call a "state banquet," attended by all of the nation's dignitaries.

The following questions will help you discover the facts contained in this chapter of Daniel.

Sample Helping Questions

1. Describe the setting of this chapter as stated in verse 1.

DANIEL 5:1-31 5

2. In the first four lessons, you were given questions that helped you to outline the passages that you were studying. By this time in your study, you should be able to outline the passage for yourself. Do not be afraid of making a mistake. Your attempt to outline the story will help you to wrestle with the text. Write your outline below. (Note: The number of lines may or may not match the number of sections in your outline.)

3. What was Daniel's position in Babylon during the reign of Belshazzar?

5 Lesson Five

4. Belshazzar's servants brought forth the golden vessels that Nebuchadnezzar had stolen from the Jerusalem Temple (2 Kings 25:15), and everyone drank from them. The word "vessels" simply means "containers," and these gold and silver containers would include bowls, pitchers, and cups. The Lord had ordered Moses to make these vessels for the tabernacle (Exodus 25:29). Why do you think Belshazzar chose to drink from of the Temple vessels? What do you suppose he was trying to say with that choice?

5. Before Daniel gives Belshazzar the message, he first compares him to King Nebuchadnezzar. What are the points of similarity and the points of difference between Belshazzar and Nebuchadnezzar?

6. How does Daniel apply the "handwriting" to Belshazzar? What does it mean for him and for his kingdom?

DANIEL 5:1-31   5

7. What teaching would we draw from this text in regard to the worship of idols? (See verse 4.)

8. What do the queen's words reveal about Daniel's reputation?

9. Daniel's very blunt response to Belshazzar in verse 17 is different from his previous politeness when he had addressed King Nebuchadnezzar. Why do you think Daniel's attitude changed?

10. How was Daniel's message to Belshazzar fulfilled in verses 30-31?

Lesson Five

Now, it is your turn to build on the facts that have been discovered already. You can do this by making up some of your own Helping Questions for Daniel 5:1-31.

Your Helping Questions

DANIEL 5:1-31 **5**

Your Helping Questions have discovered many more facts in Daniel 1:1-21. Here are a few more questions that may not have come to mind. Consider these additional questions now.

1. In verses 18-21, what major points does Daniel make to the king?

2. In verses 22-23, what specific charges does Daniel bring against Belshazzar?

3. What was Daniel's reward for interpreting the handwriting on the wall?

DISCERN

As you worked through the Discover step of the previous section, you noticed many important facts contained in Daniel 5:1-31. Now is the time to gather up all the helping tools that you have used thus far and apply them to this biblical text. By selecting relevant symbols and marking systems, you are embedding the truth of the Bible deeper into your heart and mind. Continue to think creatively as you use

Lesson Five

your helping tools. By doing this you are tagging specific truths contained in the text with something that you have developed on your own. This will help you remember the Word as well. We need the Holy Spirit to guide us when studying God's Word; therefore, let us pause for prayer.

PAUSE for PRAYER

Lord God, I pray that You would open my eyes to the glory and wonder of Your Word. I ask that You would pour out Your grace and thereby produce genuine change in my life. Please allow the seeds from Scripture to bear real, noticeable fruit in tangible acts of sacrificial love for others. Help me to follow the advice of James 1:22, which says, "Be ye doers of the word, and not hearers only, deceiving your own selves" (AKJV). Enable me to hear the full message from Your Word, so that it will shape and direct my practical living. In the wonderful name of Jesus, I pray. Amen.

→PULLING IT ALL TOGETHER←

The Helping Questions in the Discover and Discern sections of your study have helped you to get a close-up view of Daniel chapter 5. Now, you need a widescreen view of everything that you have learned so far. You need to get the big picture of what you have learned in the Discern section; so reread all your Helping Questions and answers. The following comments and guiding questions will help you to bring into focus the message of this important chapter of the Bible.

1. How does chapter 5 reinforce the lesson conveyed by King Nebuchadnezzar in chapter 4?

_____
_____
_____
_____
_____
_____

DANIEL 5:1-31 | 5

2. The words "tasted the wine" are more accurately translated "influenced by the wine," implying at least partial drunkenness. The influence of alcohol can cause a person to commit unwise acts. Sponsoring a banquet while the Persian army was encamped near Babylon shows Belshazzar's contempt for the enemy's power. Having become intoxicated, however, his arrogance pushes him even further. He shows contempt for the power of God by calling for the gold and silver vessels from God's Temple in Jerusalem so that he and his guests might drink wine from the sacred goblets. ==Arrogance toward other human rulers is bad, but arrogance toward Almighty God raises the offense to a higher level.== ✱

3. The fingers that wrote on the wall were not literally "human," but they looked like human fingers. God is a spirit, but He can take on human form whenever He deems it necessary. Other important references to the finger of God include Exodus 8:19, Psalm 8:3 (and Exodus 31:18, which describes the stone tablets of the covenant as inscribed "by the finger of God"). Why do you think that God chose to make His "finger" visible?

4. Why do you think the writing appeared near the lampstand?

Lesson Five

5. After the handwriting appeared on the wall, a helpful suggestion was offered by the newly arrived "queen," who had not been present during the banquet. We read earlier that the king's "wives" were drinking with him, so who is this queen? The word "queen" can also mean "queen-mother," that is, the mother of the king. In Babylon (and in Israel), the queen-mother held a very influential position as advisor to her son. Like every good mother, she came in when she heard the commotion, and she attempted to calm her son.

Praise the Lord! By way of the Discover step, you have grappled with a very dramatic and very sobering chapter of the Bible. With the help of God and the Holy Spirit, you have been drawn into the heart of God and His work through Daniel in the time of the Babylonian exile.

Reread all that you have learned from Daniel 5:1-31. You might want to jot down some notes on a separate piece of paper to keep track of all the facts revealed by the Discover step. Now organize these truths of the Bible and write them out in the following Summarize Your Findings section.

Summarize Your Findings

DANIEL 5:1-31

You can now put together everything that you have learned and write out your interpretation of this passage. Do not worry that your interpretation may be different from someone else's interpretation. There is more than one way of describing the teachings of this biblical text, and just the activity of putting your thoughts into words will help you to remember the message of Daniel.

5 Lesson Five

Your Interpretation

You are now in a very good position to write out a biblically informed interpretation of Daniel 5:1-31. In this step, you will record your interpretations of this chapter of Daniel in the areas of Christian beliefs, practices, and spirituality. How does this biblical text inform our beliefs regarding the nature and character of God, the plans and purposes of God, the doctrines of salvation, sanctification, the baptism of the Holy Spirit, sin, healing, the last days, the family, the Church, etc.? Are there issues in this text that you do not understand or that cause you to be uncomfortable? Explain how this text may impact spiritual topics like prayer, fasting, witnessing, testimony, giving, study, worship, sacraments, etc. Write down any interpretations that relate to our beliefs, practices, or spirituality. What does it mean that God holds our "life-breath" (verse 23)?

Give some thought and prayer to all that has been revealed in your study up to now, and write out your interpretation in the space provided.

Daniel 5:1-31

King Belshazzar should have learned from the experience of Nebuchadnezzar; but, instead, he "lifted himself up" against Almighty God. Belshazzar became proud, just like Nebuchadnezzar. However, Belshazzar's arrogance even exceeded that of Nebuchadnezzar. His desecration of the holy vessels from God's Temple in Jerusalem was a greater crime than anything done by his predecessors. Daniel continues his rebuke by pointing to Belshazzar's idolatry. While he and his guests praised the lifeless idols of Babylon, he failed to give any glory to Almighty God who holds everyone's breath in His hand and who directs everyone's pathways. With one accusation after another, Daniel lays out God's case against Belshazzar. In paraphrase, Daniel says, "You knew what God has done in the past, but you ignored it. You exalted yourself, desecrated God's holy things, and disregarded the power of God." Belshazzar does not take God seriously. He does not really believe that God holds in His hand the breath of life.

According to some commentators, the words "MENE MENE TEKEL UPHARSIN" could refer to three different pieces of money: the mina, the shekel and the half-mina. This is a possibility, but Daniel translates the words in a different way. The word "MENE" means "to count out" or "to number;" therefore, the days of Belshazzar's rule have been numbered, and they have come to an end. It is significant that Daniel uses the past tense—Belshazzar's rule has already been numbered and ended—it is a sure thing. The word "TEKEL" means "to weigh," and Daniel understands that God does the weighing. God has weighed Belshazzar on the scales and has found something lacking in him. God has decided that Belshazzar is not fit to rule; therefore, God takes the kingdom from him. The word "UPHARSIN" means "divided" or "cut in two." Because Belshazzar is not fit to rule, God has divided the Babylonian Empire and has given it to the Medes and the Persians.

Even though Daniel had earlier refused the king's rewards, they were given to him anyway. He is clothed with royal robes and gold jewelry, and he is exalted to be third ruler in the kingdom. Ironically, however, his position in the Babylonian Empire would last only a few hours, because Babylon would fall to the enemy that very night. Daniel's prophecy came to pass immediately. That night, Darius the Mede invaded Babylon and killed King Belshazzar. Apparently, Darius was the head of the Persian army during the rule of the emperor Cyrus (see 2 Chronicles 36:22-23; Ezra 1:1-8; Isaiah 45:1; Daniel 1:21).

You may want to consult with your Bible dictionaries or encyclopedias to learn more about king Belshazzar and his queen-mother (5:10). They can be found online here:

Belshazzar, https://www.blueletterbible.org/search/Dictionary/viewTopic.cfm?topic=ET0000519

Queen-mother, https://www.blueletterbible.org/search/Dictionary/viewTopic.cfm?topic=IT0007199

Lesson Five

Devote

As you enter into this Devote section, remember that just as Daniel was a *faithful witness* in the midst of challenging times in a foreign land, every believer must be willing to do the same. We are called to be faithful in whatever circumstances face us.

In this step of our Bible study, you strengthen your relationship to God. It is not enough to read and study the Bible—we must devote ourselves to serving and worshiping the God of the Bible. It is time to allow the Holy Spirit to speak to you on a deeper level. Basically, you should ask, "God, in light of what You have taught me in Your Word, what do You want me to do?" As you Devote yourself to teachings contained in Daniel 5:1-31, prayerfully consider the following:

1. By now you have become very familiar with this chapter of Daniel. Therefore, you are ready to let the passage speak to your heart, if you have not already done so. In this step, you should write down the effect this passage has on you as a believer. How does it make you feel? What emotions are brought to the surface as you read the text? Do you feel gratitude, joy, hope, love, heaviness, conviction, guilt, liberty, awe, amazement, or courage?

_____
_____
_____
_____

2. Are there any idols in your life that hinder your relationship to God? Have you failed to give God the glory that He deserves? What do you want to do in response to this text?

_____
_____
_____
_____
_____

DANIEL 5:1-31   5

3. How has this text affected you? Do you sense a transformation of your heart? Do you desire a certain kind of transformation?

_____
_____
_____
_____
_____
_____

PAUSE for PRAYER

Through your inductive study of Daniel 5:1-31, you have Discovered and Discerned much about how Daniel served God as a *faithful witness*. At this point, you should pray that these powerful lessons become real in your own life. You might want to pray something like this:

> Heavenly Father, I thank You for all the marvelous things You have done through this study of Daniel. Thank You for Your love that has been revealed to me and for the love that is shared together in Your body, the Church. I pray that You will watch over all the words that You have sown into my heart today. Protect these words and cause them to take root and produce wonderful things, things of beauty and great blessings to many. As I come to the close of this lesson, make me alert to the voice of the Holy Spirit. Yours is the kingdom, the power, and the glory, in this age and forevermore. Amen.

DISCIPLE

Belshazzar had believed that he and his people were safe behind their impenetrable walls of stone. However, the enemy created a clever scheme that enabled them to enter the city. The Euphrates River ran underneath the walls of Babylon and through the center of the city. The enemy dug a canal that diverted enough water away from the city that they were able to sneak under the walls where the river had been. Some ancient documents declare that Babylon was taken without a fight. The lesson is, "Therefore let him who thinks he stands take heed lest he fall" (1 Corinthians 10:12).

Christians would not knowingly and willingly profane the holy things of God, but our lack of watchfulness can cause us to unintentionally offend God. Sometimes we take for granted the sacred presence

5 Lesson Five

of God and the things of God. For example, God dwells within us through the Holy Spirit, but we can grow so accustomed to the Spirit that we become ungrateful. Furthermore, because the Bible is readily available to us, we may fail to appreciate its unique power and influence.

God is not pleased when people profane holy things. In the Book of Genesis, Esau profaned his birthright by selling it for a bowl of soup (Genesis 25:34; Hebrews 12:16). Moses became angry and profaned the Lord by striking the rock when God had told him to speak to the rock. Moses was a great man, but God judged him for his sin (Numbers 20:8-12).

In the New Testament, we read that the Jewish people had allowed the sacred Temple to be profaned: "And Jesus went into the temple of God, and cast out all them that sold and bought in the temple, and overthrew the tables of the moneychangers, and the seats of them that sold doves, and said unto them, It is written, My house shall be called the house of prayer; but ye have made it a den of thieves" (Matthew 21:12-13 KJV).

The Church is a sacred institution, and we must be careful that we do not dishonor God by our disrespectful behavior in the Church of God (1 Corinthians 11:22). Regarding the Church, the apostle Paul writes, "Know ye not that ye are the temple of God, and that the Spirit of God dwelleth in you? If any man defile the temple of God, him shall God destroy; for the temple of God is holy, which temple ye are" (1 Corinthians 3:16-17 KJV).

Paul speaks also of another kind of temple—the temple of our bodies. He states, "What? know ye not that your body is the temple of the Holy Ghost which is in you, which ye have of God, and ye are not your own? For ye are bought with a price: therefore glorify God in your body, and in your spirit, which are God's" (1 Corinthians 6:19-20, KJV). Every Christian has within them that which is holy—that which ought not to be desecrated or profaned. Our bodies are sacred vessels that contain the Spirit of God.

The Disciple step is all about taking definite steps to actualize, in concrete ways, the truths of the Bible. The Disciple step is about bringing the will of God down to our own life context. It should be remembered that the genuine principles of the kingdom of God cannot be brought to pass in our own strength. Spiritual growth must be empowered by the Holy Spirit. So, in prayer and through the Holy Spirit, the following points can serve as guidelines for you to actualize the challenges of this lesson.

This week, I will respond to Daniel 5:1-10 in these specific ways:

1. I will honor God by showing respect to His house, to His people (the Church), to His Word (the Bible), and to His temple (my body).

2. I will remain sober minded at all times, living under the influence of the Holy Spirit (Ephesians 5:18-20).

DANIEL 5:1-31 5

3. I will be a faithful witness to everyone around me.

4. When God reveals one of my faults, I will repent immediately and seek for purity of heart and holiness of life.

The Great Commission of Jesus (Matthew 28:18-20) commands us to go into all the world and make disciples. This is an important part of your personal discipleship. You must follow in the footsteps of Daniel and be a faithful witness at all times. By maintaining a faithful witness, we help to fulfill the Great Commission.

Enliven Encountering God Through His Word

LESSON SIX

DANIEL
6:1-28

FAITHFUL WITNESS OF GOD'S DELIVERANCE

Lesson Six

DANIEL 6:1-28

LESSON SIX

DANIEL 6:1-28

Faithful Witness of God's Deliverance

KEY VERSE

He delivers and rescues and performs signs and wonders in heaven and on earth, who has also delivered Daniel from the power of the lions (Daniel 6:27).

Introduction

At the end of Daniel 5, we learned that Babylon was conquered by Darius, who was apparently a general under Cyrus, the emperor of the Persian Empire. Therefore, Daniel, now about 85 years of age, is facing the transition to a new and different kingdom. Historians tell us that Cyrus would negotiate with the leaders of the nations that he conquered; and, if they were willing to submit to his authority, he would allow them to continue in positions of leadership. Therefore, when he appointed 120 administrators and three governors to direct the affairs of Babylon (Daniel 6:1-2), Daniel was able to continue as one of the three governors who had authority over the kingdom.

However, Daniel's faith and integrity were soon tested. The 120 administrators and the two other governors soon became jealous of Daniel's outstanding performance. After all, he was not a native Babylonian. He was an outsider, one of the captives from Judah; and his Babylonian colleagues considered him to be an intruder and a usurper of their authority. Therefore, they devised a plan to get rid of him by taking advantage of the new king's lack of familiarity with Daniel and with Daniel's history in Babylon.

In this lesson, you will dig into the familiar story of Daniel and the lions' den. Through the steps of inductive Bible study, you will find treasures of truth that you have never seen before now. You will

6 LESSON SIX

learn how Daniel became a "Faithful Witness to God's Deliverance," and you will learn how to be a *faithful witness* whenever your own faith is tested. Remember the profound words of the apostle Paul, who wrote, "God is faithful, who will not allow you to be tempted beyond what you are able, but with the temptation will provide the way of escape also, that you may be able to endure it" (1 Corinthians 10:13).

PAUSE for PRAYER

Let us pause for prayer, asking God for wisdom and insight as we study the Scripture. At the end of your prayer, read and meditate on the following words from Psalm 119.

> Let Your mercies come also to me, O Lord—Your salvation according to Your word.
> So shall I have an answer for him who reproaches me, for I trust in Your word.
> And take not the word of truth utterly out of my mouth, for I have hoped in Your ordinances.
> So shall I keep Your law continually, forever and ever.
> And I will walk at liberty, for I seek Your precepts.
> I will speak of Your testimonies also before kings, and will not be ashamed.
> And I will delight myself in Your commandments, which I love.
> My hands also I will lift up to Your commandments, which I love, and I will meditate on Your statutes" (Psalm 119:41-48 NKJV).

In the wonderful name of Jesus, we pray. Amen.

THE TEXT

Daniel 6:1-28

¹It seemed good to Darius to appoint 120 satraps over the kingdom, that they would be in charge of the whole kingdom, ²and over them three commissioners (of whom Daniel was one), that these sa-

Daniel 6:1-28

traps might be accountable to them, and that the king might not suffer loss. [3] Then this Daniel began distinguishing himself among the commissioners and satraps because he possessed an extraordinary spirit, and the king planned to appoint him over the entire kingdom. [4] Then the commissioners and satraps began trying to find a ground of accusation against Daniel in regard to government affairs; but they could find no ground of accusation or *evidence of* corruption, inasmuch as he was faithful, and no negligence or corruption was *to be* found in him. [5] Then these men said, "We will not find any ground of accusation against this Daniel unless we find *it* against him with regard to the law of his God."

[6] Then these commissioners and satraps came by agreement to the king and spoke to him as follows: "King Darius, live forever! [7] All the commissioners of the kingdom, the prefects and the satraps, the high officials and the governors have consulted together that the king should establish a statute and enforce an injunction that anyone who makes a petition to any god or man besides you, O king, for thirty days, shall be cast into the lions' den. [8] Now, O king, establish the injunction and sign the document so that it may not be changed, according to the law of the Medes and Persians, which may not be revoked." [9] Therefore King Darius signed the document, that is, the injunction.

[10] Now when Daniel knew that the document was signed, he entered his house (now in his roof chamber he had windows open toward Jerusalem); and he continued kneeling on his knees three times a day, praying and giving thanks before his God, as he had been doing previously. [11] Then these men came by agreement and found Daniel making petition and supplication before his God. [12] Then they approached and spoke before the king about the king's injunction, "Did you not sign an injunction that any man who makes a petition to any god or man besides you, O king, for thirty days, is to be cast into the lions' den?" The king replied, "The statement is true, according to the law of the Medes and

Lesson Six

Persians, which may not be revoked." ¹³ Then they answered and spoke before the king, "Daniel, who is one of the [exiles from Judah, pays no attention to you, O king, or to the injunction which you signed, but keeps making his petition three times a day."

¹⁴ Then, as soon as the king heard this statement, he was deeply distressed and set his mind on delivering Daniel; and even until sunset he kept exerting himself to rescue him. ¹⁵ Then these men came [l]by agreement to the king and said to the king, "Recognize, O king, that it is a law of the Medes and Persians that no injunction or statute which the king establishes may be changed."

¹⁶ Then the king gave orders, and Daniel was brought in and cast into the lions' den. The king spoke and said to Daniel, " Your God whom you constantly serve will Himself deliver you." ¹⁷ A stone was brought and laid over the mouth of the den; and the king sealed it with his own signet ring and with the signet rings of his nobles, so that nothing would be changed in regard to Daniel. ¹⁸ Then the king went off to his palace and spent the night fasting, and no entertainment was brought before him; and his sleep fled from him.

¹⁹ Then the king arose at dawn, at the break of day, and went in haste to the lions' den. ²⁰ When he had come near the den to Daniel, he cried out with a troubled voice. The king spoke and said to Daniel, "Daniel, servant of the living God, has your God, whom you constantly serve, been able to deliver you from the lions?" ²¹ Then Daniel spoke to the king, "O king, live forever! ²² My God sent His angel and shut the lions' mouths and they have not harmed me, inasmuch as I was found innocent before Him; and also toward you, O king, I have committed no crime." ²³ Then the king was very pleased and gave orders for Daniel to be taken up out of the den. So Daniel was taken up out of the den and no injury whatever was found on him, because he had trusted in his God. ²⁴ The king then gave orders, and

DANIEL 6:1-28

they brought those men who had maliciously accused Daniel, and they cast them, their children and their wives into the lions' den; and they had not reached the bottom of the den before the lions overpowered them and crushed all their bones.

²⁵ Then Darius the king wrote to all the peoples, nations and *men of every* language who were living in all the land: "May your peace abound! ²⁶ I make a decree that in all the dominion of my kingdom men are to fear and tremble before the God of Daniel; For He is the living God and enduring forever, and His kingdom is one which will not be destroyed, and His dominion *will be* forever. ²⁷ "He delivers and rescues and performs signs and wonders in heaven and on earth, Who has *also* delivered Daniel from the power of the lions."

²⁸ So this Daniel enjoyed success in the reign of Darius and in the reign of Cyrus the Persian.

DANIEL IN THE DEN OF LIONS—BY DANIEL BRITON RIVIEREN

LESSON SIX

DISCOVER

Recall the main purpose of the Discover step of inductive Bible study. The Discover step is all about digging out the most important facts contained in the text. One cannot begin to interpret a passage in the Bible without first knowing the central ideas contained in the section under review. This is where the Who? What? When? Where? Why? and How? questions come into play. They help us get a handle on the important facts set forth in the Bible. The answers to the Helping Questions build a firm foundation for an informed interpretation of the Scriptures that you will give later in the study.

Sample Helping Questions

1. As in lesson five, you should attempt to outline the passage for yourself. Do not be afraid of making a mistake. Your work in outlining the story will help you to wrestle with the text. Write your outline below. (Note: The number of lines may or may not match the number of sections in your outline.)

DANIEL 6:1-28 | 6

2. How is Daniel's character and performance described in Daniel 6:1-3?

3. Why does Daniel's faithfulness and integrity pose a challenge to his fellow administrators?

4. What do Daniel's enemies think is their only chance of catching Daniel doing something wrong (verses 4-5)?

5. Daniel's enemies persuade the king to prohibit anyone making a petition to any God or man other than King Darius. What does this action imply about their knowledge of Daniel's life?

Lesson Six

6. How does Daniel respond to the King's new law (verse 10)?

7. In order to avoid being arrested, Daniel could have prayed in secret. Instead, he continued his normal routine, opening his window toward Jerusalem, and praying openly. Why was he so bold?

8. What do Daniel's enemies learn about him in verse 11?

9. King Darius is disturbed by the fact that Daniel has been caught in a trap. However, he puts Daniel in the lion's den anyway. How does the text show that King Darius is not happy about his decision?

DANIEL 6:1-28 | 6

10. What are most significant actions and attitudes of the king after he cast Daniel into the lions' den (verses 18-20)?

11. Look at Daniel's reply to the king in verses 21-22, what do you think is most important about Daniel's reply?

Your Helping Questions

Create some of your own Helping Questions that will enable you to Discover the treasures that can be found in Daniel chapter 6.

Lesson Six

DANIEL 6:1-28   6

Discern

The Discern step is one of the most creative steps in our inductive Bible study. So, take a moment to review all the helping tools that you have created in previous lessons. Personalized consistency adds power to your symbols, underlining, and highlighting of important portions of the text. By "owning" the marking system that you have created and by using these symbols in the same way, you can see their meaning at a glance. That is, after you have worked inductively through a portion of the Bible, you can skim down the page and get the main ideas just from the helping tools that you have developed. Also, repeated use of a symbol or color will help "imprint" this upon your mind and heart making it easier to recall the meaning in the future.

By now, you realize that a good inductive study is like an ongoing devotion that is bathed in prayer. It is a continual invitation of the Holy Spirit to illumine our hearts and minds to the meaning of the Bible. Take a moment to invite the Holy Spirit to guide you in the application of your helping tools.

Pause *for* Prayer

You may want to begin your prayer by reciting these words from Saint Ephraim:

> Lord, who can grasp all the wealth of just one of your words? What we understand is much less than we leave behind, like thirsty people who drink from a fountain. For your word, Lord, has many shades of meaning just as those who study it have many different points of view. The Lord has colored His word with many hues so that each person who studies it can see in it what He loves. He has hidden many treasures in His word so that each of us is enriched as we meditate on it. The word of God is a tree of life that from all its parts offers you fruit that is blessed. It is like that rock opened in the desert that from all its parts gave forth a spiritual drink."

In the wonderful name of Jesus, we pray. Amen.

6 Lesson Six

→Pulling It All Together←

Look back through all your Helping Questions and all the symbols and highlighting of your helping tools. Take note of all the facts that you have uncovered and any special emphases, repetitions, and parallel sayings in this section. See if you can Discern the main message of Daniel chapter 6. You will want to pull it all together here in an effort to make an informed interpretation later on.

Here are a few questions that may help you in putting together your facts.

1. The name *Daniel* means "God is my judge." Explain how God's deliverance of Daniel from the lions' den affirms Daniel's name.

2. In verses 21–22, Daniel explains the reason why God delivered him from the lion's den. What reasons did Daniel give? Does Daniel's statement surprise you in any way?

3. King Darius offers a different reason for God delivering Daniel. What reason does King Darius give?

DANIEL 6:1-28   6

4. How are the events at the end of this chapter (especially verse 28), similar to the endings of the previous chapters? Is it possible that God's preservation of His people is a theme of the Book of Daniel? How would you state that theme in your own words?

5. Cyrus the Persian is mentioned in verse 28. Read the following Scriptures and explain why Cyrus is important: 2 Chronicles 36:22-23; Ezra 1:1-3.

6. In the ancient Near East, anyone who made a false charge would be punished by receiving the same sentence they had sought for their victim. Read Deuteronomy 19:16-21, Esther 8:7, and Proverbs 26:27; and explain why Daniel's enemies were thrown into the lion's den.

7. Compare the words of King Darius in 6:25-27 to words spoken by King Nebuchadnezzar in 4:1-3 and 34-35. How are they similar?

Lesson Six

You may want to look back to chapter 3, where you investigated the meaning of the word "satrap," which is also found in Daniel 6:1-4. If you see any other difficult words in chapter 6, look them up in a dictionary or online.

Summarize Your Findings

DANIEL 6:1-28

6

Your Interpretation

In this step, you will record your interpretations of this chapter of Daniel in the areas of Christian beliefs, practices, and spirituality. How does this biblical text inform our beliefs regarding the nature and character of God, the plans and purposes of God, the doctrines of salvation, sanctification, the baptism of the Holy Spirit, sin, healing, the last days, the family, the Church, etc.? Are there issues in this text that you do not understand or that cause you to be uncomfortable? Explain how this text may impact spiritual topics like prayer, fasting, witnessing, testimony, giving, study, worship, sacraments, etc. Write down any interpretations that relate to our beliefs, practices, or spirituality. The following questions may help you with your interpretation:

1. What does God's deliverance of Daniel reveal about who God is?

2. Another topic of importance in Daniel 6 is the ministry of angels. Angels play a significant role in the Bible (see Hebrews 1:14). Sometimes angels are sent as messengers, but at other times God sends angels to protect His people (see Psalm 34:7). The protective role of angels is demonstrated in Daniel chapter 6 when God sends an angel to shut the mouths of the lions (verse 22). See also 2 Kings 6:17; Acts 5:19-20; 27:23-25; and Psalm 91:11.

3. King Darius recognizes that Daniel's deliverance is the working of God's "signs and wonders" (verse 27). Signs and wonders are God's way of bearing witness to His presence and direction in the world (Hebrews 2:4). What can we learn about signs and wonders from Daniel 6?

4. We should not overlook the fact that King Darius is much distressed by the situation and even fasts and prays through a sleepless night (verse 18). This shows that even people who are not believers have a conscience. What can we learn about the conscience from Daniel 6?

Lesson Six

Your Interpretation Continued

DANIEL 6:1-28 | 6

Devote

In this step of our Bible study, you strengthen your relationship to God. It is not enough to read and study the Bible—we must devote ourselves to serving and worshiping the God of the Bible. It is time to allow the Holy Spirit to speak to you on a deeper level. Basically, you should ask, "God, in light of what You have taught me in Your Word, what do You want me to do?" As you enter into this Devote section, consider the following:

1. By now you have become very familiar with this chapter of Daniel. Therefore, you are ready to let the passage speak to your heart, if you have not already done so. In this step, you should write down the effect this passage has on you as a believer. How does it make you feel? What emotions are brought to the surface as you read the text? Do you feel gratitude, joy, hope, love, heaviness, conviction, guilt, liberty, awe, amazement, or courage?

_____

_____

_____

_____

_____

_____

_____

_____

2. We can learn much from Daniel's example. Daniel is certainly trustworthy, faithful, and courageous. He is also steadfast in prayer, even though he knows that his prayer will cause him to be cast into the den of lions. How do you want to change in response to Daniel's example?

_____

_____

Lesson Six

3. How has this text affected you? Do you sense a transformation of your heart? Do you desire a certain kind of transformation? Verse 28 reminds us that Daniel remains in captivity. In truth, Daniel's entire life is spent in the lions' den of the exile; and God has delivered him from the lions over and over. What kind of lions' den are you in?

DANIEL 6:1-28

6

PAUSE for PRAYER

The following prayer is inspired by Saint Benedict of Nursia. It is a great way to begin your prayer today as you seek for God's help in making Daniel 6 come alive in your own life.

> Gracious and holy Father, give us the wisdom to discover you, the intelligence to understand you, the diligence to seek after you, the patience to wait for you, eyes to behold you, a heart to meditate on you, and a life to proclaim you, through the power of the Spirit of Jesus, our Lord. Amen

DISCIPLE

There are three main parties at work in Daniel chapter 6.

First is Daniel, who is a man of integrity and faithful to his duties, a man who is described as without fault. Even on close examination, none can find any reason to accuse him. Therefore, he is entrapped and then punished for being a righteous person. He is "suffering for righteousness sake" (1 Peter 3:14). Although his enemies try to destroy him, God delivers him.

The second party might be described as Daniel's colleagues, who become his enemies. They are determined to get rid of Daniel, even though he is an innocent and honorable man. How would you describe the evil forces that cause people to treat an innocent person as they treated Daniel?

The third party involved is Darius the king, who is misled into playing a role in the unjust treatment of Daniel.

Each of these parties faces choices that remind us of our own situations in life. How should we respond when one of our colleagues is promoted and we are tempted to be envious? What if that person is an immigrant? What if that person appears to be less qualified? Then, how should we respond if we are the innocent party who is being mistreated? What is the Christian response to abuse and persecution? Third, what should be our reaction to other people who attempt to include us in their schemes of manipulation against other people? How does a Christian deal with jealous, envious, dishonest, and immoral people?

Make a commitment to be faithful this week. Take the following statements as examples and then add your own.

Lesson Six

This week, I commit to:

1. Always do my best (like Daniel), so that I will develop a reputation for integrity.

2. Rejoice with my friends and coworkers who receive promotions. I will resist the temptation to be envious and jealous of them.

3. Never cooperate with people who are trying to hurt others. Instead, I will be a peacemaker (Matthew 5:9).

4. Serve God faithfully and openly, even when pressured to compromise.

5. Trust God that He will deliver me from my lion's den.

6. Forgive everyone who has plotted against me (Matthew 5:44).

Because of his courageous and prayerful lifestyle, Daniel was given the opportunity to be a "Faithful Witness of God's Deliverance." Although his enemies did not appreciate his spirituality, King Darius benefited from Daniel's witness. We never know who it is that will be most affected by our *faithful witness*. It may be a coworker, a boss, a family member, a friend, or even a total stranger.

ENLIVEN ENCOUNTERING GOD Through HIS WORD

LESSON SEVEN

DANIEL
7:1-28

FAITHFUL WITNESS OF GOD'S KINGDOM

7 Lesson Seven

Lesson Seven

Daniel 7:1-28

Faithful Witness of God's Kingdom

Key Verse

Then the sovereignty, the dominion, and the greatness of all the kingdoms under the whole heaven will be given to the people of the saints of the Highest One; His kingdom will be an everlasting kingdom, and all the dominions will serve and obey Him (Daniel 7:27).

Introduction

As we wrote earlier, whenever someone mentions the Book of Daniel, we immediately think of the story of Daniel in the lions' den, or we might remember the miraculous deliverance of the three Hebrews from the fiery furnace. These miracle stories have been told to children throughout history, and they have been popular subjects for preaching and for inclusion in Bible story books. However, the mention of Daniel may also remind us of the deep mysteries regarding the last days and the end of the world—what scholars call *eschatology* (which means the study of last things).

There is a good reason why we think of two very different subjects—miracle stories and mysteries of the end—when we reflect on the Book of Daniel. We think of Daniel in these two ways because of the format of the book itself. The Book of Daniel consists of twelve chapters. As we enter chapter 7 of Daniel, we find ourselves in new territory. The first six chapters tell a series of stories about Daniel and his friends who are in exile in Babylon. These stories are told *about* Daniel, but Daniel is not the narrator. Then, the last six chapters relate Daniel's dreams and visions regarding the future destiny of the Jewish people. These visions are recounted *by* Daniel himself.

Another difference between the first and last halves of the Book of Daniel is that the first six chapters are in chronological order, beginning with Daniel's capture by the enemy King Nebuchadnezzar, and

7 Lesson Seven

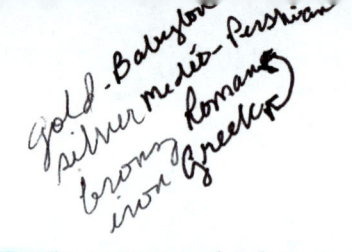

(handwritten note: Gold—Babylon, Silver—Medo-Persian, Bronze—Romans, Iron—Greeks)

ending with his service as an old man under the Persian King Cyrus. Chapters 7 and 8, however, are out of place chronologically, having occurred in the time between chapters 4 and 5. The historical order of the chapters would be 1, 2, 3, 4, 7, 8, 5, 6, 9, 10, 11, 12.

The miracle stories (chapters 1–6) demonstrate clearly that God is able to care for His people even when they are in very difficult and challenging situations. The mysteries regarding the end (chapters 7–12) show us that God is in control of world history; therefore, we should not worry about the future or be paralyzed with fear. As God's people, we can maintain a *faithful witness* to the world of unbelievers if we will trust in God's goodness and if we will live in the knowledge that the end is near. In His care for us and in His governance of the world, God is sovereign.

PAUSE for PRAYER

Lord Jesus, send Your Spirit to help us to read the Scriptures just as You sent Your Spirit to inspire the writing of the Scriptures. In the light of the Word, help us to discover the presence of God in the events of our lives. Just as the cross seemed to be the end of all hope but became the source of life and of resurrection, so let the trials and tests of our lives result in joy and hope for us. Create in us silence so that we may listen to Your voice in the Scriptures, in events and in people, and in those who are poor and suffering. May Your Word guide us so that we may experience the force of Your resurrection and witness to others that You are alive in our midst as source of love, healing, and peace. We ask this of You, Heavenly Father, in the name of Jesus Christ, Your Son. Amen.

THE TEXT

Daniel 7:1-28

¹In the first year of Belshazzar king of Babylon Daniel saw a dream and visions in his mind as he lay on his bed; then he wrote the dream down and related the following summary of it. ² Daniel said, "I was looking in my vision by night, and behold, the four winds of heaven were stirring up the great sea. ³ And four great beasts were coming up from the sea, different from one another. ⁴ The first was like

DANIEL 7:1-28   7

a lion and had the wings of an eagle. I kept looking until its wings were plucked, and it was lifted up from the ground and made to stand on two feet like a man; a human mind also was given to it. ⁵And behold, another beast, a second one, resembling a bear. And it was raised up on one side, and three ribs *were* in its mouth between its teeth; and thus they said to it, 'Arise, devour much meat!' ⁶After this I kept looking, and behold, another one, like a leopard, which had on its back four wings of a bird; the beast also had four heads, and dominion was given to it. ⁷After this I kept looking in the night visions, and behold, a fourth beast, dreadful and terrifying and extremely strong; and it had large

Lion with Wings
by Lee Roy Martin

Bear with Ribs in Its Mouth
by Lee Roy Martin

Leopard with Four Heads
by Lee Roy Martin

Beast with Ten Horn and Iron Teeth
by Lee Roy Martin

iron teeth. It devoured and crushed and trampled down the remainder with its feet; and it was different from all the beasts that were before it, and it had ten horns. ⁸While I was contemplating the horns,

137

7 LESSON SEVEN

behold, another horn, a little one, came up among them, and three of the first horns were pulled out by the roots before it; and behold, this horn possessed eyes like the eyes of a man and a mouth uttering great *boasts*.

⁹ "I kept looking until thrones were set up, and the Ancient of Days took *His* seat; His vesture *was* like white snow and the hair of His head like pure wool. His throne *was* ablaze with flames, its wheels *were* a burning fire. ¹⁰ "A river of fire was flowing and coming out from before Him; thousands upon thousands were attending Him, and myriads upon myriads were standing before Him; the court sat, and the books were opened. ¹¹ Then I kept looking because of the sound of the boastful words which the horn was speaking; I kept looking until the beast was slain, and its body was destroyed and given to the burning fire. ¹² As for the rest of the beasts, their dominion was taken away, but an extension of life was granted to them for an appointed period of time. ¹³ "I kept looking in the night visions, and behold, with the clouds of heaven one like a Son of Man was coming, and He came up to the Ancient of Days and was presented before Him. ¹⁴ "And to Him was given dominion, glory and a kingdom, that all the peoples, nations and *men of every* language might serve Him. His dominion is an everlasting dominion which will not pass away; and His kingdom is one which will not be destroyed.

DISCOVER

The focus of the Discover step is to uncover the facts contained in the passage we are studying. These facts will be revealed to you as you answer the questions: Who? What? When? Where? and How? All the facts that you discover will feed into your interpretation later on. Reread Daniel 1:1-21 and answer the following sample Helping Questions.

DANIEL 7:1-28   7

Sample Helping Questions

1. As in lessons five and six, you should attempt to outline chapter seven for yourself. Do not be afraid of making a mistake. Your work in outlining the vision will help you to wrestle with the text. Write your outline below. (Note: The number of lines may or may not match the number of sections in your outline.)

2. According to verse 1, when did Daniel's dream take place? What other background details can you name?

Lesson Seven

3. Other prophets wrote down their revelations (Isaiah 8:1, 16; 30:8; Jeremiah 30:2; 36:2; 51:60; Ezekiel 43:11; Habakkuk 2:2). Why do you suppose that Daniel wrote down the dream immediately?

4. How many beasts came out of the turbulent sea? Describe each one.

5. The beasts in the vision are symbolic, and their horns are also symbolic. In the Bible, horns represent power and authority. They sometimes signify powerful leaders also (Daniel 7:24). Therefore, what does it mean that a little horn replaced three other horns?

6. How do the ten horns relate to Nebuchadnezzar's dream (see Daniel 2:41-42)?

DANIEL 7:1-28 7

7. The vision of the Ancient of Days and His court bears strong resemblance to other visions of God that we find in Isaiah, Ezekiel, and Revelation. Purity, holiness, and majesty are the three most prominent characteristics of Daniel's vision of God. Purity and holiness are indicated by the white garments, by the hair like wool, and by the fiery throne and stream. God's majesty is evident throughout the vision, but it is especially prominent in the large number of worshipers who stood before Him to give Him honor (verse 10). What other elements of the courtroom scene in verses 9-10 do you think are important?

8. What happens to the "little horn" in verse 11 after the record books are opened in verse 10?

9. What happens to the other beasts in verse 12? Why do you suppose they were not cast into the fire with the fourth beast?

Lesson Seven

9. Describe the kingdom of the "Son of Man."

10. These scenes of terrible beasts disturbed Daniel and grieved him in his spirit. The beasts were frightful, and Daniel was anxious to know what the dream meant. Confused and dazed, Daniel looked around and saw heavenly messengers standing nearby, so he asked one of them to reveal the meaning of the dream. The messenger willingly explained the interpretation to Daniel. What do the beasts represent? (see verse 17)

11. The four beasts represent four kingdoms (verse 17). We are not told the names of the kingdoms, and Bible scholars do not agree regarding the identity of the kingdoms. Many Bible scholars identify the four kingdoms as Babylon, Media, Persia, and Greece; but others believe they are Babylon, Media-Persia, Greece, and Rome. Why does Daniel not tell us the names of the kingdoms that are represented by these beasts? Do the beasts appear to correspond to the statue in Nebuchadnezzar's dream (chapter 2)? If so, explain the correspondence.

12. According to verse 18, who will possess the kingdom? For how long?

13. Daniel is not quite satisfied with this brief interpretation; therefore, he requests more information regarding the fourth beast in particular (verse 19). He then sees the little horn making war against God's people and even prevailing against them (verse 21) until the war is interrupted by the coming of the "Ancient of Days." The expression "Ancient of Days" refers to a person who is very old; consequently, in biblical culture, they would also be thought of as very wise. This person is God himself, and He is later called the "Most High" (verse 25). The Ancient of Days has the power and authority to exercise judgment and to give the kingdom to the . . . "saints." When the text says that "judgment was given to the . . . saints," it means that judgment was rendered in favor of the saints and against the little horn. How long will the little horn be allowed to rule (verse 25–26)?

14. Summarize the powerful conclusion to the vision as stated in verse 27.

Lesson Seven

Your answers to the sample Helping Questions have uncovered many facts about Daniel 7:1-28. Yet there is much more to be discovered in this chapter. Develop your Helping Questions to draw forth even more information from this valuable vision of Daniel.

Your Helping Questions

DANIEL 7:1-28 | 7

DISCERN

The Discern step will give more clarity, order, and insight into the message of Daniel chapter 7. Quickly skim over all the helping tools that you have used in the previous lessons. These consist of the underlining, symbols, highlighting, etc. that you have used to mark your text. A lot of space has been left between the lines of the text so that you can really accentuate words that are repeated, contrasting ideas, and special word pictures that might be found in this section. When you are finished with your marking up the text, patterns and emphases will begin to surface. All this will lead to a more informed interpretation later.

It was mentioned in the introduction that parts of Daniel, especially chapters 7–12, are eschatological; that is, they concern the last things. Furthermore, Daniel is a particular type of eschatological literature that is called *apocalyptic*. The word *apocalyptic* means an "unveiling" or an "uncovering" of secret mysteries. The Book of Revelation is also included in the category of apocalyptic literature. Apocalyptic literature is different from other types of prophecy, because it includes visions of heaven, visits by angels, representations of symbolic creatures, the figurative use of numbers, and predictions of God's sudden and powerful intervention to bring about His kingdom on earth. Apocalyptic prophecies like those of Daniel speak to us when our faith has been challenged and when the normal structures of the community are either threatened or have collapsed. Therefore, apocalyptic represents a crisis literature; and it is intended to offer comfort and hope to the afflicted.

Furthermore, apocalyptic writings point to spiritual realities that are unseen by the natural eye. For example, heaven may be unseen, but it is real. Also, all earthly powers, though inflicting much pain, will soon be reduced to insignificance in the ultimate sense. God has promised to intervene in history and to impose His rule upon the earth. Apocalyptic literature such as Daniel was relevant for the ancient audience, and it is relevant for us today.

This kind of writing speaks a powerful word to three different audiences.

(1) To the oppressed, deprived, and alienated, apocalyptic literature describes God's alternative order, which will free them from the one under which they now suffer.

(2) To the oppressors, who are obstructing God's order of compassion and justice, it speaks a warning.

(3) To the wavering—the ones who cannot decide whether to trust fully in God or to trust in human powers—this genre serves as a "Wake up!" call.

7 Lesson Seven

Before you access your collection of helping tools and bring them to bear on Daniel 7:1-28, let us pause for prayer. It is vitally important that we hear from God as we attempt to interpret His word.

Pause for Prayer

After praying in your own words, read the following passage from Psalm 119, in which the psalmist restates a commitment to serve God and follow God's Word.

> Remember the word to Your servant, upon which You have caused me to hope.
> This is my comfort in my affliction, for Your word has given me life.
> The proud have me in great derision, yet I do not turn aside from Your law.
> I remembered Your judgments of old, O Lord, and have comforted myself.
> Indignation has taken hold of me because of the wicked, who forsake Your law.
> Your statutes have been my songs in the house of my pilgrimage.
> I remember Your name in the night, O Lord, and I keep Your law.
> This has become mine, because I kept Your precepts.
> You are my portion, O Lord; I have said that I would keep Your words.
> I entreated Your favor with my whole heart; be merciful to me according to Your word.
> I thought about my ways, and turned my feet to Your testimonies.
> I made haste, and did not delay to keep Your commandments.
> The cords of the wicked have bound me, but I have not forgotten Your law.
> At midnight I will rise to give thanks to You, because of Your righteous judgments.
> I am a companion of all who fear You, and of those who keep Your precepts.
> The earth, O Lord, is full of Your mercy; teach me Your statutes (Psalm 119:49-64 NKJV).

In the wonderful name of Jesus, we pray. Amen.

→Pulling It All Together←

You have done a lot of work in your Helping Questions and helping tools. It is time to pull it all together so that you can render your best interpretation of Daniel 7:1-28. Remember, all your work should flow into that one, major interpretation that you will give later on. Keep that in mind as you pull things together.

DANIEL 7:1-28   7

Here are a few more questions that will help you summarize your findings to this point.

1. In his vision, Daniel is by the sea, and the wind is blowing from every direction. The "great sea" is the Mediterranean Sea. In ancient times, the sea was a symbol of chaos and destructive evil. In the Old Testament, God blasts the sea with His rebuke (see Psalm 18:15); He sets a guard over the sea (Job 7:12; Jeremiah 5:22); He causes the sea to dry up (Nahum 1:4); He treads on the sea (Habakkuk 3:15); and He fights the sea monsters (Isaiah 27:1).

2. The four winds of heaven (Daniel 7:2) often represent creative power. The word "wind" is ruach, and it can also be translated "spirit." It is the "Spirit," the ruach of God that blows over the waters of the original creation (Genesis 1:2). It is the "east wind" (ruach) that divides the Red Sea so that Israel can cross on dry ground. The prophet Ezekiel calls upon the "four winds" (ruach) to breathe life into the dry bones of Israel. The striving of the four winds means that God is at work, and His power lies behind the following activities.

3. The speech of the "little horn" is described in similar terms in verses 8, 11, 20, and 25. Can you see the similarity? Describe the repetition and what it means. The little horn is not identified by name, but more information about him will be revealed in chapters 8–12.

Lesson Seven

4. Nebuchadnezzar is compared to a lion (Jeremiah 4:7; 49:19; 50:17) and his armies to an eagle because of their swiftness (Ezekiel 17:3; Habakkuk 1:8). How do these Scripture references add to your interpretation of Daniel's vision?

5. Compare Daniel 7:4 to Nebuchadnezzar's experience of becoming like an animal in chapter 4. Do you see a correspondence? What are the correspondences?

6. Review Nebuchadnezzar's dream in Daniel chapter 2. Do you see the parallels between parts of the statue in Daniel 2 and the four beasts in Daniel 7?

Daniel 7:1-28

Quickly scan your Helping Questions, helping tools, and Pulling It All Together sections. Summarize all your findings in the space provided below.

Summarize Your Findings

7 Lesson Seven

Your Interpretation

In this step, you will record your interpretations of this chapter of Daniel in the areas of Christian beliefs, practices, and spirituality. How does this biblical text inform our beliefs regarding the nature and character of God, the plans and purposes of God, the doctrines of salvation, sanctification, the baptism of the Holy Spirit, sin, healing, the last days, the family, the Church, etc.? Are there issues in this text that you do not understand or that cause you to be uncomfortable? Explain how this text may impact spiritual topics like prayer, fasting, witnessing, testimony, giving, study, worship, sacraments, etc. Write down any interpretations that relate to our beliefs, practices, or spirituality.

The following questions might get you started:

1. Reflect on the name "Ancient of Days." What does it mean and what effect does it have on you to meditate on it?

2. The kingdom of God is described in verses 17 and 27. Have these verses been fulfilled, or are they yet to be fulfilled in the future? Is there a spiritual kingdom of God now?

DANIEL 7:1-28   7

3. Consider the repetition of the terms "heaven," "kingdom," "dominion," and "saints." How does this repetition impact our view of the future?

4. In verse 25, we find the phrase "time, times, and half a time," which seems to indicate 3 ½ years. Do you think this number is meant to be literal or symbolic? Why?

5. In Daniel's vision, the "little horn" . . . (1) opposes God, and (2) opposes God's people. What does this tell us about the spirit behind the "little horn"?

Lesson Seven

Your Interpretation Continued

DANIEL 7:1-28   7

Devote

In this step of our Bible study, you strengthen your relationship to God. It is not enough to read and study the Bible—we must devote ourselves to serving and worshiping the God of the Bible. It is time to allow the Holy Spirit to speak to you on a deeper level. Basically, you should ask, "God, in light of what You have taught me in Your Word, what do You want me to do?" As you enter into this Devote section, consider the following:

1. By now you have become very familiar with this chapter of Daniel. Therefore, you are ready to let the passage speak to your heart, if you have not already done so. In this step, you should write down the effect this passage has on you as a believer. How does it make you feel? What emotions are brought to the surface as you read the text? Do you feel gratitude, joy, hope, love, heaviness, conviction, guilt, liberty, awe, amazement, or courage?

_____

_____

_____

_____

_____

_____

_____

_____

2. What do you want to do in response to this text?

_____

_____

_____

_____

Lesson Seven

3. How has this text affected you? Do you sense a transformation of your heart? Do you desire a certain kind of transformation?

Pause for Prayer

At this point, you should pray that the Holy Spirit will take the message of Daniel 7 and make it real in your life. Like Daniel, we should be a "Faithful Witness of God's Kingdom," which will stand forever. The following prayer may help you to seek God in your own way:

Lord Jesus, we thank You for the Word that has enabled us to understand better the will of the Father. May Your Spirit enlighten our actions and grant us the strength to practice what Your Word has revealed to us. May we, like Daniel, not only listen to the Word, but also practice the Word. You who live and reign with the Father in the unity of the Holy Spirit forever and ever. Amen.

In the wonderful name of Jesus, we pray. Amen.

DANIEL 7:1-28

⳨ DISCIPLE

Some people try to live in the past. Adjusting to change is difficult for them, and they long for days gone by. It is true that we are products of the past and that we should remember everything that God has done for us. However, it is one thing to remember and honor the past, but it is quite another thing to live in the past. The apostle Paul advises us to put the past behind us and to press forward for the goal that is in front of us (see Philippians 3:14).

Other people have an unhealthy obsession with the future. Their interest in the Bible is limited to the study of the last days, and they have little concern for discipleship and faithful living. Certainly, we should be noticing the signs of the times, and we should be eagerly awaiting the return of Jesus. However, Jesus emphasized that we must work until He comes.

Neither living in the past nor obsession with the future is the proper stance for the Christian. With proper honoring of the past and with proper anticipation of the return of Jesus, the Christian lives faithfully in the present time (2 Peter 3:14; 1 John 3:3; 1 Thessalonians 5:6).

Daniel understood both the heritage of his past and God's plan for the future. In light of these two perspectives, he walked with God in the midst of severe opposition. This lesson's study of Daniel 7 has opened up new insights about the future, and these insights will enable us to follow Daniel's example of walking by faith in this present world so that we may be "Faithful Witnesses of God's Kingdom."

After his dream, Daniel understood more about the future than he did before he went to bed that night, but he still did not understand everything. Mysteries remained, and Daniel continued to be alarmed and cautious. Like Daniel, we are living in perilous times, and we are admonished to be awake, observant, prayerful, faithful, and working for the Master. Jesus says, "Take heed, watch and pray; for you do not know when the time is" (Mark 13:33 NKJV). The apostle Peter encourages us to be diligent while we wait for the Lord's return: "Therefore, beloved, looking forward to these things, be diligent to be found by Him in peace, without spot and blameless" (2 Peter 3:14 NKJV).

This week, I commit to:

1. Trusting in God's sovereignty over the world.

2. Living in anticipation of Christ's soon return.

3. Praising God for His faithfulness.

4. Humbly serving God as I witness to those around me.

ENLIVEN ENCOUNTERING GOD Through HIS WORD

LESSON EIGHT

DANIEL

8:1-27

FAITHFUL WITNESS OF THE LAST DAYS

8 Lesson Eight

Daniel 8:1-27

Lesson Eight

Daniel 8:1-27

Faithful Witness of the Last Days

Key Verse

And the vision of the evenings and mornings which has been told is true; but keep the vision secret, for it pertains to many days in the future (Daniel 8:26).

Introduction

The visions of Daniel are good news; however, they contain a large amount of troubling information. They tell us that arrogant human rulers will continue to arise and oppose God and the people of God. They tell us that persecution is inevitable, and believers will sometimes die for their faith. The Book of Daniel gives courage and perseverance to God's people who are suffering. The message of Daniel helps us to "endure to the end" (Matthew 24:13). Daniel, himself, is a captive who lives in a foreign land and who is subject to the whims and wishes of enemy rulers (see Philippians 3:20). Daniel knows that God is sovereign and that the eternal kingdom of God will eventually be established on earth. Nevertheless, the troubles of this present age are so disturbing to Daniel that he becomes physically ill (Daniel 8:27; see Matthew 24:9-10). Like Abraham, Daniel was looking for a city, "whose builder and maker is God" (Hebrews 11:10 NKJV).

In Daniel 8:1-27, Daniel is a "Faithful Witness of the Last Days." The vision of chapter 8 is a restatement and expansion of Daniel's dream from chapter 7. The dreams and visions of Daniel build upon each other, chapter-by-chapter, until we finally get the complete picture by the end of the book. As we read through the Book of Daniel, we must be patient, so that we can absorb each part of the message as it is revealed in each chapter.

8 LESSON EIGHT

PAUSE for PRAYER

Before reading Daniel 8:1-27, let us pause for prayer, asking God for the aid of His Holy Spirit.

O, Lord, I come to Your Word with an open heart and an open mind. Fill me with Your Holy Spirit, which is the Spirit of wisdom. Fill me with the knowledge of the Word of God. Fill me with every kind of spiritual wisdom and intelligence, so I am able to understand the Word of God in depth. Help me to understand the message of Daniel 8:1-27. Holy Spirit, I need You to continually mold me into the figure and the form of Jesus. Open my heart and my mind, so that I may truly hear the Word of God. In the wonderful name of Jesus, I pray. Amen.

THE TEXT

Daniel 8:1-27

¹In the third year of the reign of Belshazzar the king a vision appeared to me, Daniel, subsequent to the one which appeared to me previously. ²I looked in the vision, and while I was looking I was in the citadel of Susa, which is in the province of Elam; and I looked in the vision and I myself was beside the Ulai Canal. ³Then I lifted my eyes and looked, and behold, a ram which had two horns was standing in front of the canal. Now the two horns *were* long, but one *was* longer than the other, with the longer one coming up last. ⁴I saw the ram butting westward, northward, and southward, and no *other* beasts could stand before him nor was there anyone to rescue from his power, but he did as he pleased and magnified *himself*.

⁵While I was observing, behold, a male goat was coming from the west over the surface of the whole earth without touching the ground; and the goat *had* a conspicuous horn between his eyes. ⁶He came

DANIEL 8:1-27

up to the ram that had the two horns, which I had seen standing in front of the canal, and rushed at him in his mighty wrath. ⁷I saw him come beside the ram, and he was enraged at him; and he struck the ram and shattered his two horns, and the ram had no strength to withstand him. So he hurled him to the ground and trampled on him, and there was none to rescue the ram from his power. ⁸Then the male goat magnified *himself* exceedingly. But as soon as he was mighty, the large horn was broken; and in its place there came up four conspicuous *horns* toward the four winds of heaven. ⁹Out of one of them came forth a rather small horn which grew exceedingly great toward the south, toward the east, and toward the Beautiful *Land*. ¹⁰It grew up to the host of heaven and caused some of the host and some of the stars to fall to the earth, and it trampled them down. ¹¹It even magnified *itself* to be equal with the Commander of the host; and it removed the regular sacrifice from Him, and the place of His sanctuary was thrown down. ¹²And on account of transgression the host will be given over *to the horn* along with the

Ram With Two Horns
by Lee Roy Martin

Goat With Prominent Horn

8 Lesson Eight

regular sacrifice; and it will fling truth to the ground and perform its will and prosper. ¹³ Then I heard a holy one speaking, and another holy one said to that particular one who was speaking, "How long will the vision about the regular sacrifice apply, while the transgression causes horror, so as to allow both the holy place and the host to be trampled?" ¹⁴ He said to me, "For 2,300 evenings and mornings; then the holy place will be properly restored."

¹⁵ When I, Daniel, had seen the vision, I sought to understand it; and behold, standing before me was one who looked like a man. ¹⁶ And I heard the voice of a man between *the banks of* Ulai, and he called out and said, "Gabriel, give this *man* an understanding of the vision." ¹⁷ So he came near to where I was standing, and when he came I was frightened and fell on my face; but he said to me, "Son of man, understand that the vision pertains to the time of the end."

¹⁸ Now while he was talking with me, I sank into a deep sleep with my face to the ground; but he touched me and made me stand upright. ¹⁹ He said, "Behold, I am going to let you know what will occur at the final period of the indignation, for *it* pertains to the appointed time of the end.

²⁰ The ram which you saw with the two horns represents the kings of Media and Persia.

²¹ The shaggy goat *represents* the kingdom of Greece, and the large horn that is between his eyes is the first king. ²² The broken *horn* and the four *horns that* arose in its place represent four kingdoms *which* will arise from *his* nation, although not with his power.

²³ "In the latter period of their rule, when the transgressors have run *their course*, a king will arise, insolent and skilled in intrigue. ²⁴ "His power will be mighty, but not by his *own* power, and he will destroy to an extraordinary degree and prosper and perform *his will*; he will destroy mighty men and the holy

DANIEL 8:1-27

people. ²⁵ "And through his shrewdness he will cause deceit to succeed by his influence; and he will magnify *himself* in his heart, and he will destroy many while *they are* at ease. He will even oppose the Prince of princes, but he will be broken without human agency. ²⁶ "The vision of the evenings and mornings which has been told is true; but keep the vision secret, for *it* pertains to many days *in the future*." ²⁷ Then I, Daniel, was exhausted and sick for days. Then I got up *again* and carried on the king's business; but I was astounded at the vision, and there was none to explain *it*.

DISCOVER

By now you are familiar with the Discover step. The following Helping Questions are designed to *dis*-cover the facts and truths contained in Daniel 8:1-27. Again, just focus on the content of the passage and do not worry about the meaning at this point. Recall that the operative word for the discover step is *observation*. You should bring all your powers of observation to bear on this text; therefore, get in a setting where you can completely focus on the Bible. As you answer the Helping Questions, be mindful of key ideas or facts that might emerge as you work along. The quality of the work that you do here will enhance the quality of your interpretation later on.

Sample Helping Questions

The following questions will help you discover the facts contained in this chapter of Daniel.

1. Read through chapter eight and attempt to outline the story for yourself. Do not be afraid of making a mistake. Your work in outlining the passage will help you to wrestle with the text. Write your outline below. (Note: The number of lines may or may not match the number of sections in your outline.)

_____

_____

_____

_____

8 LESSON EIGHT

2. Daniel's first revelation came through a dream, which means that he was asleep. However, this second revelation came by means of a "vision," which signifies that he was awake when the vision appeared before him. Daniel's second revelation comes to him approximately two years after his first. In what year of Belshazzar's reign does the vision occur?

3. Daniel lived in Babylon, but in his vision, he was inside the fortress in Shushan (also called Susa). Shushan was the capital of the province of Elam, 200 miles east of Babylon. A century after the time of Daniel, the Persian king Xerxes built a splendid palace there. Who was cupbearer to the king in Shushan? (See Nehemiah 1:1-2.) Where does the Book of Esther take place? (See Esther 1:1-3.)

4. While Daniel's dream in chapter 7 was framed in terms of hybrid, grotesque animals, the animals in the vision of chapter 8 appear in their natural form (with some unusual features). What is the first animal that Daniel sees? What is unusual about its appearance?

DANIEL 8:1-27

5. The word "considering" means that Daniel was attempting to understand the meaning of what he had just seen. He was trying to discern the significance of the vision. However, while he was thinking on it, he saw a second animal. What was the second animal that Daniel saw? What is unusual about its appearance and its behavior?

6. Describe how the goat approaches the ram.

7. What happened to the ram when it was attacked by the goat? Describe the result of their battle.

8. What happened to the goat after it defeated the ram and it became strong? How did its horns change?

165

LESSON EIGHT

9. As in chapter 7, Daniel sees the rise of a "small horn" or "little horn" that grew until it became "exceeding great" (verse 9). Describe the expansion of the little horn's empire. In which directions did it grow?

10. How did Daniel respond to the vision (verse 15)?

11. Who was sent to give Daniel the interpretation of the vision (verses 16-17)?

12. What was Daniel's response to the appearing of Gabriel in verse 17? Why did he respond that way?

DANIEL 8:1-27   8

13. In verses 20-21, Gabriel names the historical meaning of the ram and the goat. This is more information than we have received up to this point in Daniel. What nations do they represent?

14. The meaning of the "small horn" (verse 9) is given to Daniel in verses 23-25. Describe the characteristics of the new leader that arises in these verses.

15. According to verse 24, the small horn "will be mighty." However, what is the significance of the phrase "but not by his own power"?

As you have worked through this passage, you have no doubt thought of some additional Helping Questions. Therefore, bring your creativity to bear on Daniel 8:1-27 by developing your own Helping Questions. Develop those questions that will lift out the important facts and ideas of this passage. Remember, when you think of a good question, do your best to answer that question as well. This will force your mind to grapple with the words Daniel uses in chapter 8. In this way, you will be "inducted" or drawn into the message of the chapter. You will then be able to render an interpretation that is true to the inspiration Daniel received from the Holy Spirit.

8 Lesson Eight

Your Helping Questions

DANIEL 8:1-27 | 8

DISCERN

After answering all the Helping Questions, you should have a pretty good grasp on the main features contained in Daniel 8:1-27. The discern step will grant you even more insight into this wonderful portion of the Bible. By now, you know how to proceed with this special aspect of the inductive study. So, review all the helping tools that you have developed thus far. Take note again of the color coding, highlighting, and symbol making that you have used to this point. Apply these marking elements to the copy of the text included in this lesson. Try to be consistent in your application of your highlighting and symbols; but, above all, be creative.

If you see any difficult words or concepts in the biblical text, use your Bible dictionary, Google, Wikipedia, or the other resources listed at the beginning of this book to look up their meanings.

It is important to quiet our thoughts prior to applying the Design step to this special passage. Let us pause for prayer and seek the spiritual guidance as we continue to study.

PAUSE *for* PRAYER

The following prayer from Psalm 119 will help you to focus your prayer. After repeating these words of the psalmist, continue to pray in your own words.

> Your hands have made me and fashioned me; give me understanding, that I may learn Your commandments.
> Those who fear You will be glad when they see me, because I have hoped in Your word.
> I know, O Lord, that Your judgments are right, and that in faithfulness You have afflicted me.
> Let, I pray, Your merciful kindness be for my comfort, according to Your Word to Your servant.
> Let Your tender mercies come to me, that I may live; for Your law is my delight.
> Let the proud be ashamed, for they treated me wrongfully with falsehood; but I will meditate on Your precepts.
> Let those who fear You turn to me, those who know Your testimonies.

Lesson Eight

Let my heart be blameless regarding Your statutes, that I may not be ashamed.

My soul faints for Your salvation, but I hope in Your word.

My eyes fail from searching Your word, saying, "When will You comfort me?"

For I have become like a wineskin in smoke, yet I do not forget Your statutes.

How many are the days of Your servant? When will You execute judgment on those who persecute me?

The proud have dug pits for me, which is not according to Your law.

All Your commandments are faithful; they persecute me wrongfully; help me!

They almost made an end of me on earth, but I did not forsake Your precepts.

Revive me according to Your lovingkindness, so that I may keep the testimony of Your mouth (Psalm 119:73–88 NKJV).

In the wonderful name of Jesus, we pray. Amen.

→Pulling It All Together←

Now is the point in your study when you gather up all the facts that you found in the Discover step and take note of all of the patterns and emphases that you noted in the Discern step. Reread these sections prayerfully, asking the Holy Spirit to guide you to an informed and relevant interpretation of Daniel 8:1-27. In summary, everything that you have done to this point should flow into the interpretation that you will give below. You have worked hard, so do not rush to the next step or you will waste some of the rich insights that you have gained into this passage.

You have worked hard in the Discover and the Discern steps of inductive study. One thing you have learned for sure is that Daniel 8:1-27 is an incredibly rich portion of Scripture. It is packed with wisdom and truth. However, it is a challenge to get a handle on all of it. This next section will help you do just that. Take a moment to reread Daniel 8, and carefully study all that you have learned thus far. You may want to have a notepad handy to write down all the facts that have arisen as a result of your work. Summarize them in the following Summarize Your Findings section.

Daniel 8:1-27

Summarize Your Findings

8 Lesson Eight

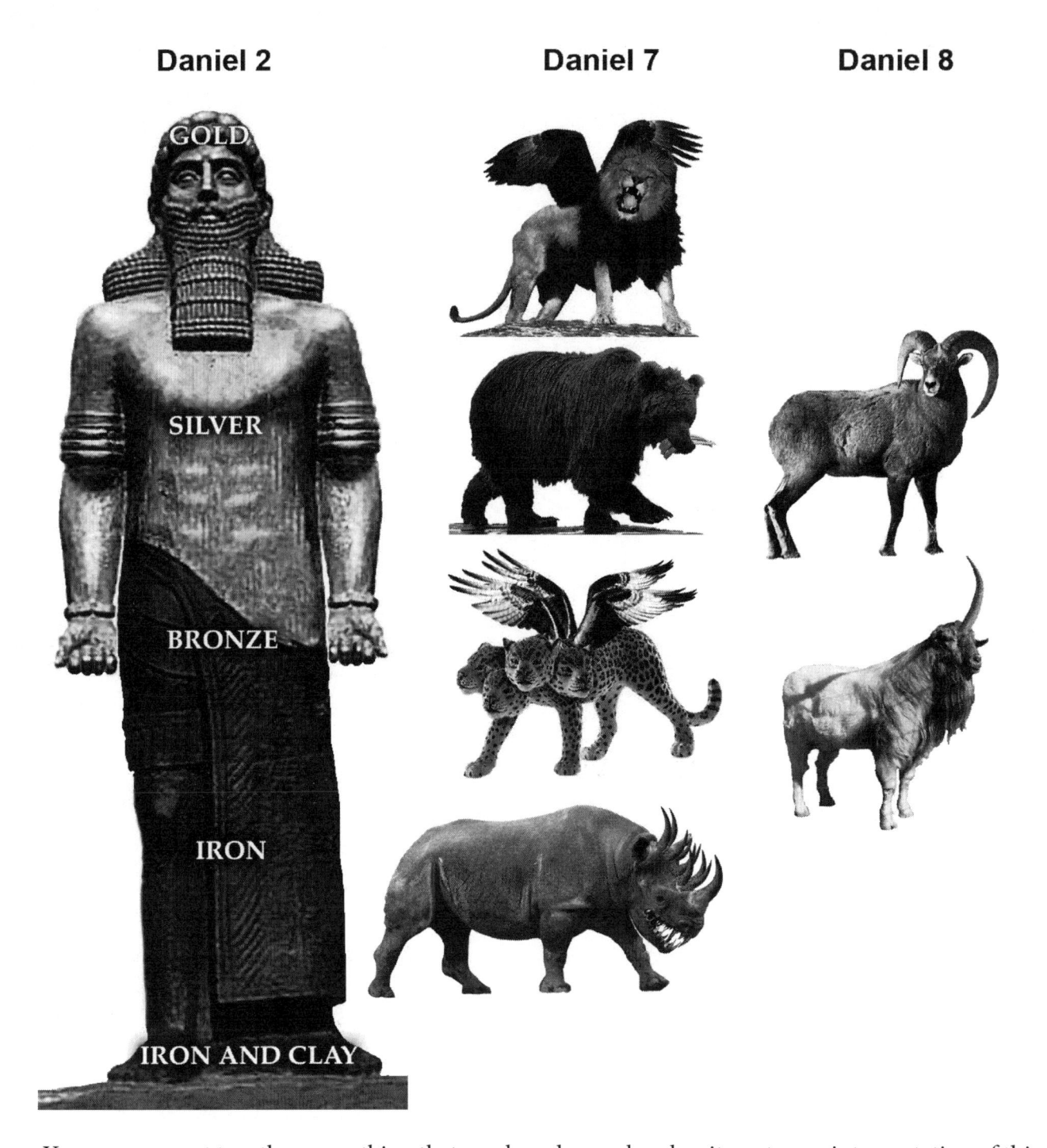

Daniel 2 **Daniel 7** **Daniel 8**

You can now put together everything that you have learned and write out your interpretation of this passage. Do not worry that your interpretation may be different from someone else's interpretation. There is more than one way of describing the teachings of this biblical text, and just the activity of putting your thoughts into words will help you to remember the message of Daniel.

DANIEL 8:1-27

In this step, you will record your interpretations of this chapter of Daniel in the areas of Christian beliefs, practices, and spirituality. How does this biblical text inform our beliefs regarding the nature and character of God, the plans and purposes of God, the doctrines of salvation, sanctification, the baptism of the Holy Spirit, sin, healing, the last days, the family, the Church, etc.? Are there issues in this text that you do not understand or that cause you to be uncomfortable? Explain how this text may impact spiritual topics like prayer, fasting, witnessing, testimony, giving, study, worship, sacraments, etc. Write down any interpretations that relate to our beliefs, practices, or spirituality.

Your Interpretation

Lesson Eight

Devote

In this step of our Bible study, you strengthen your relationship to God. It is not enough to read and study the Bible—we must devote ourselves to serving and worshiping the God of the Bible. It is time to allow the Holy Spirit to speak to you on a deeper level. Basically, you should ask, "God, in light of what You have taught me in Your Word, what do You want me to do?" As you enter into this Devote section, consider the following:

1. By now you have become very familiar with this chapter of Daniel. Therefore, you are ready to let the passage speak to your heart, if you have not already done so. In this step, you should write down the effect this passage has on you as a believer. How does it make you feel? What emotions are brought to the surface as you read the text? Do you feel gratitude, joy, hope, love, heaviness, conviction, guilt, liberty, awe, amazement, or courage?

2. What do you want to do in response to this text?

DANIEL 8:1-27   8

3. How has this text affected you? Do you sense a transformation of your heart? Do you desire a certain kind of transformation?

_____
_____
_____
_____
_____
_____
_____
_____
_____
_____

Pause for Prayer

Daniel 8:1-27 has given us much to think about and much to pray about. Before we enter into the Disciple step, let us take time to ask for God's help in applying the Word of God to our daily lives. You should pray in your own words, but you may want to begin with the following prayer of David. He wrote,

> Create in me a clean heart, O God, and renew a steadfast spirit within me. Do not cast me away from Your presence, and do not take Your Holy Spirit from me (Psalm 51:10-11).

In the wonderful name of Jesus, we pray. Amen.

Disciple

At this point, I want to offer a bit of commentary on the symbolism found in Daniel's vision. According to verse 20, the ram with two horns represents the two kingdoms of Media and Persia. The longer horn, which came up last, is Persia. A zodiac list from the first century names Aries, the ram, as the astrological symbol of Persia, and the Persian army carried a gold ram's head. The expansion of the Persian Empire eventually made it the greatest on earth at that time.

8 Lesson Eight

The goat is named in verse 21 as Greece, and the large horn between its eyes is Alexander the Great, the first king of the Greek Empire. Alexander came from the west (verse 5) and defeated the Persians in 330 BC. In the vision, he approached the ram, and "ran unto him in the fury of his power" (verse 6 KJV). The violence of the attack is emphasized by the three words "ran," "fury," and "power." He ran rather than marched. His attack was not calm and calculating, but was furious or angry. The word "power" can mean "might" or "strength," and here it means that the goat attacked with great rage. Verse 7 repeats the fact that the goat (Greece) attacked the ram (Persia). The goat attacked the ram with all his might, striking the ram and shattering both its horns. The ram was not just defeated; he was thrown to the ground and trampled by the goat. There was no other kingdom that could give aid to the ram. He was utterly defeated.

The goat (Greece) became very great, symbolizing the fact that the Greek Empire was the most extensive empire to have arisen up to that point in history. However, "when he was strong," that is, at the height of his power "the great horn was broken." And so it happened with Alexander the Great, that he died unexpectedly at the age of 32 after he had extended his kingdom all the way to India. Four horns grew up in the place of the one horn (verses 8 and 22), as the kingdom was divided into sections. This was fulfilled when Alexander died, and the Greek Empire was divided between his generals.

Out of one of the four horns came another "small horn" (verse 9). This one king expanded toward the south (Egypt), the east (Persia), and toward the "beautiful land." The beautiful land, which could also be translated "glorious land" (ESV), refers to Judea and the city of Jerusalem (Ezekiel 20:6, 15). It is at this point that the vision becomes more intense and personal for Daniel. The small horn attacks Jerusalem and even brings down some of the "host of heaven" (v. 10).

The word "host" means "army," and the host of heaven usually refers to the angels of God. However, this vision uses symbolism (such as the ram and the goat); therefore, the "host of heaven" refers to the Jewish people in Jerusalem who are serving God. By casting down "some of the host and some of the stars," the small horn is trampling upon the Jewish people.

The small horn exalts himself against the "commander of the host," who is God (v. 11). Through his military might, the small horn forces the priests out of the Temple and forbids them from offering sacrifices there. Therefore,

Alexander the Great

176

DANIEL 8:1-27

8

the "sanctuary was thrown down," meaning that the Jerusalem Temple was desecrated and dishonored. The small horn will "fling truth to the ground." For the Jews, the truth is found in the Torah, the Law of Moses.

The small horn is not given a name, but Bible scholars agree he is Antiochus IV Epiphanes, who took control of the portion of the Greek Empire that included Judea. Antiochus claimed to be a god, and he forbade Jewish religious practices and required everyone to worship the Greek god Zeus. In verse 11, we read "it removed the regular sacrifice." The decree of Antiochus Epiphanes in 1 Maccabees 1:45 forbids "burnt offerings and sacrifices and drink offerings in the sanctuary." The offering of the sacrifices was prevented by the installation of a pagan altar upon the altar of burnt offerings in the Temple (1 Maccabees 1:59). Read Exodus 29:38-42 and Numbers 28:2-8 and find what sacrifices are required daily. Daniel 8:14 states that the sacrifices would be taken away for 2,300 days, which corresponds to the time from the murder of the High Priest Onias III in 171 BC to the rededication of the Temple in 164 BC. The rededication of the Temple is commemorated in the Jewish festival of Hanukkah. You can read about the rededication in the Book of Maccabees 4:36-59

Coin with Likeness of Antiochus IV Epiphanes

The description of him as "understanding of dark sentences" implies what we might call an evil genius. Antiochus was intelligent, skilled in intrigue, and characterized by duplicity. He was a ruthless, malicious, spiteful leader who showed pity to no one. Antiochus became powerful, and he would "magnify himself," which means that he would have delusions of grandeur. However, his power was not "his own"—his power was given to him by Almighty God, and it would be taken away by Almighty God. He would decimate the "holy people," which was fulfilled when Antiochus killed 80,000 Jews in 168 BC.

Further descriptions of Antiochus (which also describe the beast of the last days) are:

(1) He will "cause craft to prosper" (KJV). The word "craft" means "deceit;" thus, the meaning is that he will make treachery succeed;

(2) He will "magnify himself" (KJV), meaning that he will grow exceedingly arrogant;

(3) He "by peace shall destroy many" (KJV). The words "by peace" refer to the fact that the Jews thought themselves to be living in safety and peace. Antiochus would attack them without warning when they thought they were safe.

Lesson Eight

(4) He will "stand up against the Prince of princes" (KJV). In Hebrew, the word "prince" does not mean the son of the king; rather, it is another word for the king himself. Therefore, the "Prince of princes" refers to God himself; and

(5) He will "be broken without hand" (KJV), which means that God will destroy him without using human means.

In the end, Antiochus died insane in Persia in 163 BC.

The scene changes when Daniel hears one of the saints (a believing Jew) speaking and asking, "How long will the vision be?" (v. 13 NKJV). They are not asking about the duration of the visionary experience, but the duration of the actions foretold in the vision. In other words, they are asking, "How long will this desecration last?" They ask about the absence of the "daily sacrifice," and they ask about the "transgression of desolation," which refers to Antiochus' building of an altar to Zeus in the Jerusalem Temple and offering a pig on the altar. At the same time, the "host" (people of God) are being trampled underfoot, powerless against the military might of the little horn (NKJV). The answer comes to Daniel that the sanctuary will be "cleansed" after 2300 days (6.3 years).

Gabriel informed Daniel that the vision was a description of the "time of the end" (verse 17). Whenever we hear "the end," we automatically think of the end of the world, the end of this age. In the Old Testament, however, the "end" can refer to the end of a certain period of time, such as the end of the Old Covenant and the beginning of the Messianic age, that is, the coming of Jesus the Messiah (See, for example, Isaiah 62:11; Jeremiah 5:31; Ezekiel 7:2; Habakkuk 2:3). Obviously, not all of the vision refers to the end of time. The interpretation specifically names the kingdoms of Persia and Greece, two kingdoms that were prominent before the end of the Old Testament times, but they soon disappeared. They did not persist until the end of the world.

Daniel's prophecies might be called "typological;" that is, they refer to real people and nations that existed in the past, but they also represent future people and kingdoms. The same spirit that stood behind Nebuchadnezzar, Belshazzar, Alexander the Great, and Antiochus Epiphanes also stands behind many other rulers throughout history and those in the Book of Revelation. That spirit comes from the "rulers of the darkness of this world," "spiritual wickedness in high places" (Ephesians 6:12 AKJV), and the spirit of antichrist. In fact, John tells us, "you heard that antichrist is coming, even now many antichrists have appeared" (1 John 2:18). Some elements of Daniel's prophecies were literally fulfilled during the intertestamental period. The Persian Empire arose and fell, and so did the Greek Empire. An evil general named Antiochus IV Epiphanes attacked the Jews and defiled the Temple in Jerusalem, but God gave the Jews victory and restored the Temple to its rightful place. However, these fulfilments only partially complete the picture that is painted in Daniel's dreams and visions. These visions are symbolic, prophetic, and represent a repetition of evil throughout history. The "abomination of desolation" was first committed by Antiochus, and it was repeated in AD 70 by the Romans, when they invaded Jerusalem (Matthew 24:15).

These acts, however, are also prophetic of the last days, when the same desecration will be committed before the return of Jesus (see the Book of Revelation). Old Testament prophecies often combine both short-term and long-term predictions in a way that we find difficult to separate. Like Daniel, we must seek after God for the interpretation, and we must hold the mystery until the time comes that its meaning is fully revealed.

Daniel is told that the vision is true, but that he should seal up the vision for now, but not for ever. The "evening and the morning" refers to the daily sacrifices that were offered at the beginning and end of each day. The experience overwhelmed Daniel, and he fainted. He remained ill for a number of days.

Because this vision applies to the future and because Gabriel did not fully disclose all the details, Daniel could not fully understand it, and neither can we.

This week I commit to:

1. Be thankful for the Word of God and for the presence of the Holy Spirit.
2. Trust fully in God, realizing that all the nations of the world are but a "drop from a bucket" (Isaiah 40:15) compared to the power of God.
3. Live faithfully, looking every day for the return of Jesus.
4. Put on the whole armor of God, that I may be able to stand against all the devices of the enemy (see Ephesians 6:11).

Daniel's second revelation tells us again that "evil men and impostors will grow worse and worse, deceiving and being deceived" (2 Timothy 3:13 NKJV). We are blessed to be living in the age of the Spirit, when God has given us the comfort and strength of His presence. We see wars and rumors of wars. We see famines, pestilence, floods, and earthquakes; but, we know that God will make all things new in the end. Therefore, we live in hope of a new heaven and a new earth. If we are to fulfill the Great Commission (Matthew 28:18-20), we must be "Faithful Witnesses of the Last Days."

ENLIVEN ENCOUNTERING GOD Through HIS WORD

LESSON NINE

DANIEL
9:1-27

FAITHFUL WITNESS
THROUGH PRAYER AND FASTING

9 Lesson Nine

Daniel 9:1-27

Lesson Nine

Daniel 9:1-27

Faithful Witness Through Prayer and Fasting

🔑 Key Verse

O Lord, hear! O Lord, forgive! O Lord, listen and take action! For Your own sake, O my God, do not delay, because Your city and Your people are called by Your name (Daniel 9:19).

Introduction

The events of Daniel 9:1-27 happened soon after the death of King Belshazzar, when Darius the Mede conquered Babylon (Daniel 5:31). The overthrow of Babylon and the rise of a new king caused Daniel to seek for God's wisdom and direction. As he sought God and searched the Scriptures, he came across Jeremiah's prophecy of the seventy-year exile. Jeremiah predicted that the people of Judah would be taken into captivity and would "serve the king of Babylon seventy years" (Jeremiah 25:11). He declared further, "For thus says the Lord: After seventy years are completed at Babylon, I will visit you and perform My good word toward you, and cause you to return to this place" (Jeremiah 29:10 NKJV).

This story from the life of Daniel offers strong support for the value of the written Word of God. We know that Jeremiah had made several copies of his prophecies (Jeremiah 36:4, 32; 51:60). We also know that he had contact with the exiles in Babylon and that he had shared with them the prophecy of the seventy years (Jeremiah 29:1-10). It is significant that Daniel's reading of Scripture prompted him to pray and to confess the sins of Israel. Modern Christians sometimes read the Bible only as a source of information, like an encyclopedia or like a calendar of dates and times. Regarding Daniel 9, we have focused on the "seventy years," but Daniel's response to his reading of Scripture was more personal and spiritual. He observed that the reason for the exile was the Jews' refusal to heed the warnings and

9 Lesson Nine

calls to repentance that had been issued by the earlier prophets. Because of their unfaithfulness to the covenant, they had brought upon themselves the calamity of the exile, just as it had been predicted in the law of Moses (Deuteronomy 28.49-68). Therefore, Daniel, perhaps realizing that the seventy years was near completion, began to fast and pray and confess to God the sins of his people. Our reading of Scripture should have the same kind of effect upon us (See Hebrews 4:12). The Scripture should move us to be "Faithful Witnesses Through Prayer and Fasting."

Before reading Daniel 9:1-27, let us pause for prayer and ask God to guide our thoughts and to fill our hearts with His living Word.

PAUSE for PRAYER

The following prayer may help you to seek God humbly and sincerely.

> Lord, Your Word is sweet, it is like a honeycomb, it is not hard nor is it bitter. It may burn like fire, it may be like the hammer that breaks a rock, it may be the sharp sword that pierces and separates the soul … but Lord, Your Word is sweet! Help me to listen to Your Word, that it may be gentle music, a song and an echo in my ears, my memory, and my intellect. I offer my whole being to You so that I may listen faithfully, sincerely, and strongly. Lord, let me keep my ears and heart fixed on Your voice, so that not one word may be in vain. Pour forth Your Holy Spirit to be like living water, so that my field may bear fruit, thirty, sixty, and a hundredfold. Lord, draw me to Yourself, because in You is life and light.

In the wonderful name of Jesus, we pray. Amen.

THE TEXT

Daniel 9:1-27

¹In the first year of Darius the son of Ahasuerus, by descent a Mede, who was made king over the realm of the Chaldeans— ²in the first year of his reign, I, Daniel, perceived in the books the number of years that, according to the word of the Lord to Jeremiah the prophet, must pass before the end of the desolations of Jerusalem, namely, seventy years.

DANIEL 9:1-27

³Then I turned my face to the Lord God, seeking him by prayer and pleas for mercy with fasting and sackcloth and ashes. ⁴I prayed to the Lord my God and made confession, saying, "O Lord, the great and awesome God, who keeps covenant and steadfast love with those who love him and keep his commandments, ⁵we have sinned and done wrong and acted wickedly and rebelled, turning aside from your commandments and rules. ⁶We have not listened to your servants the prophets, who spoke in your name to our kings, our princes, and our fathers, and to all the people of the land. ⁷To you, O Lord, belongs righteousness, but to us open shame, as at this day, to the men of Judah, to the inhabitants of Jerusalem, and to all Israel, those who are near and those who are far away, in all the lands to which you have driven them, because of the treachery that they have committed against you. ⁸To us, O Lord, belongs open shame, to our kings, to our princes, and to our fathers, because we have sinned against you. ⁹To the Lord our God belong mercy and forgiveness, for we have rebelled against him ¹⁰and have not obeyed the voice of the Lord our God by walking in his laws, which he set before us by his servants the prophets. ¹¹All Israel has transgressed your law and turned aside, refusing to obey your voice. And the curse and oath that are written in the Law of Moses the servant of God have been poured out upon us, because we have sinned against him. ¹²He has confirmed his words, which he spoke against us and against our rulers who ruled us, by bringing upon us a great calamity. For under the whole heaven there has not been

done anything like what has been done against Jerusalem. [13] As it is written in the Law of Moses, all this calamity has come upon us; yet we have not entreated the favor of the Lord our God, turning from our iniquities and gaining insight by your truth. [14] Therefore the Lord has kept ready the calamity and has brought it upon us, for the Lord our God is righteous in all the works that he has done, and we have not obeyed his voice. [15] And now, O Lord our God, who brought your people out of the land of Egypt with a mighty hand, and have made a name for yourself, as at this day, we have sinned, we have done wickedly.

[16] "O Lord, according to all your righteous acts, let your anger and your wrath turn away from your city Jerusalem, your holy hill, because for our sins, and for the iniquities of our fathers, Jerusalem and your people have become a byword among all who are around us. [17] Now therefore, O our God, listen to the prayer of your servant and to his pleas for mercy, and for your own sake, O Lord, make your face to shine upon your sanctuary, which is desolate. [18] O my God, incline your ear and hear. Open your eyes and see our desolations, and the city that is called by your name. For we do not present our pleas before you because of our righteousness, but because of your great mercy. [19] O Lord, hear; O Lord, forgive. O Lord, pay attention and act. Delay not, for your own sake, O my God, because your city and your people are called by your name."

[20] While I was speaking and praying, confessing my sin and the sin of my people Israel, and presenting my plea before the Lord my God for the holy hill of my God, [21] while I was speaking in prayer, the man Gabriel, whom I had seen in the vision at the first, came to me in swift flight at the time of the evening sacrifice. [22] He made me understand, speaking with me and saying, "O Daniel, I have now come out to give you insight and understanding. [23] At the beginning of your pleas for mercy a word

Daniel 9:1-27 — 9

went out, and I have come to tell it to you, for you are greatly loved. Therefore consider the word and understand the vision.

24 "Seventy weeks are decreed about your people and your holy city, to finish the transgression, to put an end to sin, and to atone for iniquity, to bring in everlasting righteousness, to seal both vision and prophet, and to anoint a most holy place. 25 Know therefore and understand that from the going out of the word to restore and build Jerusalem to the coming of an anointed one, a prince, there shall be seven weeks. Then for sixty-two weeks it shall be built again with squares and moat, but in a troubled time. 26 And after the sixty-two weeks, an anointed one shall be cut off and shall have nothing. And the people of the prince who is to come shall destroy the city and the sanctuary. Its end shall come with a flood, and to the end there shall be war. Desolations are decreed. 27 And he shall make a strong covenant with many for one week, and for half of the week he shall put an end to sacrifice and offering. And on the wing of abominations shall come one who makes desolate, until the decreed end is poured out on the desolator."

[Handwritten annotations: "49 yrs - temple destroyed"; "432 yrs. - Christ crucified"; "John the Revelator reveals more later about the Revelations"]

DISCOVER

The Discover step is when you dig into the text and learn the Who? What? When? Where? and Why? of the biblical story. It is important that you ask these questions of the text so that you can uncover (that is, "Dis-cover") the important elements in the text. Concentrate on the facts contained in this lesson and hold off on trying to draw out too much meaning at this stage. Remember, you are building a solid foundation of *what the text says* at this point and reserving *what the text means* for later in the study. So, be patient and let the process unfold, so you can feel confident when writing out your interpretation.

The following Helping Questions will guide you to discern the message of Daniel 9:1-27.

9 LESSON NINE

Sample Helping Questions

1. Read through chapter nine and attempt to outline the story for yourself. Do not be afraid of making a mistake. Your work in outlining the passage will help you to wrestle with the text. Write your outline below. (Note: The number of lines may or may not match the number of sections in your outline.)

2. When do the events of this chapter take place (verse 1)?

3. What is Daniel doing in verse 2?

DANIEL 9:1-27   9

4. What is Daniel's response to Jeremiah's prophecies (verses 3-4)?

5. How does Daniel describe God in verse 4?

6. The word "confession" signifies the acknowledgment of guilt, and it is required before forgiveness can be granted (Leviticus 5:5). Daniel's confession bears much similarity to the prayer found in Nehemiah 1:6. What confessions does Daniel make in verses 5-10?

7. Although Daniel was declared to be without fault (Daniel 6:4), he includes himself in the confession. Daniel repents on behalf of all the people of Judah who had disobeyed God's commandments, sinned against God's law, disregarded God's prophets, and trampled upon God's covenant. List the times in chapter 9 that Daniel uses the plural words "we," "us," and "our."

189

Lesson Nine

8. Why does Daniel say that Israel should be "ashamed"?

9. What is the result of Israel's sin (verses 11-14)?

10. What is the objective of Daniel's prayer? What had God done for Israel in the past that gave Daniel hope for God's mercy (verse 15)?

11. Is Daniel's prayer urgent? How can you tell (verses 16-19)?

DANIEL 9:1-27

12. Only once does Daniel use the word "forgive." Write out the verse where it occurs. The Old Testament word for forgiveness is equivalent to our idea of pardon. It means that, because of his grace, God removes the penalty for our sin.

13. In verse 21, Gabriel is called a "man," but the Hebrew word (*ish*) does not necessarily mean "human being" (that would be the Hebrew word *adam*). The Hebrew language does not have a separate word that means "person;" therefore, the word "man" can also mean "person." The fact that Gabriel comes to Daniel in swift flight should also make it clear that he is not a human being. Why did Gabriel come and speak to Daniel (verses 20-22)?

14. What indications do we see regarding God's opinion of Daniel (verse 23)?

Lesson Nine

15. Daniel had read in the prophecies of Jeremiah that Israel would be in exile for seventy years. What number does Gabriel give to Daniel, and what will be accomplished in this period of time (verse 24)?

16. The Hebrew word translated "weeks" literally means "sevens." Do you think it means seven days, seven weeks, seven months, or seven years? Describe what happens in the "sixty-two sevens" of verse 25.

17. What happens after the sixty-two sevens (verse 26)?

DANIEL 9:1-27 | 9

18. The end of the vision comes very abruptly in verse 27, with no explanation. As a reader, how does the sudden conclusion strike you? Why do you think the vision ends this way?

By working with these Helping Questions, major elements and controlling ideas have been lifted out of the text. There are many more facts and key ideas embedded in Daniel chapter 9. Take a few moments to brainstorm about some additional questions that will bring forth the facts from this important chapter of the Bible. Just by doing this exercise, you will be "drawn in" or inducted into the message of the Book of Daniel, and by extension to the mind of the Spirit that inspired Daniel to write his prophecies in the first place.

Your Helping Questions

Lesson Nine

Your Helping Questions Continued

DANIEL 9:1-27   9

DISCERN

The purpose of the Discern step is to immerse you even further into the biblical text. It is a different way to identify important features that may not have become apparent in the Discover step. You may want to take a moment and review the helping tools (symbols and marking systems) used in the previous Discern steps. Plenty of room has been left in the printed text above, so actually write out your symbols and marking systems in the spaces that are provided. Although you are free to make up some new helping tools for this lesson, you should try to use some of the symbols, highlighting, and color coding that you employed in your previous lessons. In this way, you can easily recognize repeated elements throughout the Book of Daniel and in any other book of the Bible that you might study.

If you see any difficult words or concepts in the biblical text, use your Bible dictionary, Google, Wikipedia, or the other resources listed at the beginning of this book to look up their meanings.

Before you gather all your colored pens/pencils, reconnect with the help of the Holy Spirit. Again, the Holy Spirit "shaped" the mind of Daniel when he inspired him to write these prophecies. You will be able to Discern the shape, order, or pattern of Daniel's message by using your helping tools. Once you see the pattern of Daniel's thoughts, you will gain insight into the mind of the Spirit as well.

PAUSE for PRAYER

As you work through the Discern step, allow yourself to be shaped by God's Word. Pray that you can experience God's Word like the psalmist does in this passage from Psalm 119.

> Forever, O LORD, Your word is settled in heaven.
>
> Your faithfulness endures to all generations; You established the earth, and it abides.
>
> They continue this day according to Your ordinances, for all are Your servants.
>
> Unless Your law had been my delight, I would then have perished in my affliction.
>
> I will never forget Your precepts, for by them You have given me life.
>
> I am Yours, save me; for I have sought Your precepts.
>
> The wicked wait for me to destroy me, but I will consider Your testimonies.
>
> I have seen the consummation of all perfection, but Your commandment is exceedingly broad.

Lesson Nine

> Oh, how I love Your law! It is my meditation all the day.
>
> You, through Your commandments, make me wiser than my enemies; for they are ever with me.
>
> I have more understanding than all my teachers, for Your testimonies are my meditation.
>
> I understand more than the ancients, because I keep Your precepts.
>
> I have restrained my feet from every evil way, that I may keep Your word.
>
> I have not departed from Your judgments, for You Yourself have taught me.
>
> How sweet are Your words to my taste, sweeter than honey to my mouth!
>
> Through Your precepts I get understanding; therefore I hate every false way (Psalm 119:89-104 NKJV).

In the wonderful name of Jesus, we pray. Amen.

→Pulling It All Together←

All your Helping Questions and helping tools have revealed a great amount of information. Go back and reread all the responses that you have made to your Helping Questions. Take a step back and note any repetitions, patterns, contrasts, etc. that have arisen as a result of your helping tools. Now combine all the insights that you have gained and write out a thorough summary. This exercise of Pulling It All Together will go a long way in helping to develop a very good interpretation of Daniel 9:1-27.

The following tips may help you pull everything together.

1. Take note of the various components of Daniel's prayer and fasting, giving consideration to the different words that are used to describe his activities. Compare Esther 4:3 with Isaiah 58:5.

2. Mark the repetitions of key words like "prayer"/"prayed," "supplications," "confess"/"confession," "covenant," "lovingkindness," "commandments," and "ordinances."

3. How many different ways does Daniel describe Israel's sin? That is, how many different words does he use in reference to wrongdoing and disobedience?

DANIEL 9:1-27

4. List all of the words that Daniel uses to describe God.

5. How many times is the word "desolate"/"desolation" used in chapter 9? How does the repetition of this word impact the meaning of the chapter?

6. Daniel refers to himself as the Lord's "servant" (verse 17). Use your concordance or Bible program find other Old Testament characters who were called the servant of the Lord.

7. The final verse (9:27) is clearer in the NIV translation. It reads, "He will confirm a covenant with many for one 'seven.' In the middle of the 'seven' he will put an end to sacrifice and offering. And at the Temple he will set up an abomination that causes desolation, until the end that is decreed is poured out on him." Verse 27 seems to hark back to Daniel 8:13 and to look forward to 11:31 and 12:11. Look at these four verses together and comment on how they might clarify what we have called the "abomination of desolation."

9 Lesson Nine

You have already accomplished a great deal in this lesson. Key ideas and facts have been drawn forth from your work by means of the Helping Questions. Now go back and study everything you have written up to this point. You may want to take some notes on all the things that you uncovered in the Discover step. After you have done that, summarize everything under the Summarize Your Findings section below.

Summarize Your Findings

DANIEL 9:1-27 | 9

Your Interpretation

In this step, you will record your interpretations of this chapter of Daniel in the areas of Christian beliefs, practices, and spirituality. How does this biblical text inform our beliefs regarding the nature and character of God, the plans and purposes of God, the doctrines of salvation, sanctification, the baptism of the Holy Spirit, sin, healing, the last days, the family, the Church, etc.? Are there issues in this text that you do not understand or that cause you to be uncomfortable? Explain how this text may impact spiritual topics like prayer, fasting, witnessing, testimony, giving, study, worship, sacraments, etc. Write down any interpretations that relate to our beliefs, practices, or spirituality.

9 Lesson Nine

DEVOTE

Daniel begins his prayer by addressing God as "great and awesome," terminology that emphasizes the majesty and power of God. The word "awesome" means that God is feared and worthy of reverence. Not only is God majestic, but He is also faithful to His covenant and full of mercy. After stating his confidence in God's covenant faithfulness, Daniel then proceeds to offer a detailed confession of sins, expressed through the use of six terms:

(1) "We have sinned"—sin is the general word for falling short of God's design for human behavior.

(2) We "have committed iniquity"—iniquity is to be bent, twisted, or perverted.

(3) We "have done wickedly"—wickedness consists of evil actions that proceed from an evil heart.

(4) We "have rebelled"—rebellion is the disregarding of God's clear instruction, the rejection of God's authority.

(5) "Departing from Your precepts…"—departing means "turning away from," and precepts are God's commandments.

(6) We have not "hearkened"(KJV) to the prophets who warned us (v. 6). To *hearken* is "to listen and follow through with obedience" Daniel makes no excuses. His confession is thorough and without reservation. His willingness to fast in conjunction with his prayer signifies the urgency and seriousness of his confession. The confession was not an empty ritual. Daniel's prayer is a model for us, it is the kind of confession that God desires.

Daniel pleads for forgiveness, but he pleads for more than that. His goal is the restoration of Jerusalem and the holy Temple. Jerusalem sits upon Mount Zion, which is called God's "holy mountain." Jerusalem is the City of David, Israel's great king. David brought the Tabernacle into Jerusalem; and, later, Solomon built the magnificent Temple, which Nebuchadnezzar destroyed. Daniel prays that God will remove His anger and wrath from Jerusalem and will cause His "face to shine" upon the holy sanctuary that was "desolate." The word *desolate* means "devastated." The phrase "let Your face shine" refers literally to a face that is covered with olive oil, a symbol of joy and gladness (Psalm 45:7). To make one's face to shine upon someone or something is an expression of approval and blessing (Psalm 31:16; 67:1; 80:3-19). Part of the priestly blessing was that the Lord would "make His face to shine" upon the congregation (Numbers 6:25). In His judgment upon Jerusalem, the Lord had turned away His face from the city and from His sanctuary, and they had been destroyed by the Babylonians.

The length of Daniel's prayer and fasting is not recorded, but while he continued in prayer, the angel Gabriel came to him with a message from God. This message is Daniel's third visionary experience. Daniel's prayer and fasting resulted in a visit from God's messenger and a prophecy regarding God's remedy for Israel's sin. There is no indication that Daniel prayed and fasted with the intent of receiving a visionary experience, but the experience brought Daniel to a place of humility and receptivity. Nowhere in Scripture are we commanded to seek after revelations or visions; nevertheless, prophecies and great revelations are often the results of fasting and prayer.

In verse 23, Gabriel confirms that God earnestly desires to answer Daniel's prayer. In fact, God's response was formulated as soon as Daniel began to pray (see Isaiah 65:24). The Lord is eager to answer Daniel's prayer because he is "greatly beloved," which means literally "treasured, precious." God is pleased to answer prayer, but the answer is sometimes delayed, even for the most righteous persons (Job 19:7; Psalm 22:2). Daniel is told to discern the "matter" and the "vision." (NKJV) Thus, Daniel himself must participate in the process of understanding by engaging his mind and heart. Understanding is not handed to him on a silver platter; it requires effort.

Surprisingly, Gabriel's message was not a simple declaration of forgiveness or restoration; rather, it was a mysterious prediction of "seventy weeks." The words "seventy weeks" are literally "seventy sevens," which means 490 years. Jeremiah's prediction of a seventy-year exile would be fulfilled when Cyrus, king of Persia, issued the order to rebuild Jerusalem and the Temple (2 Chronicles 36:23; Ezra 1:2-4). From that point, another 483 years remain (7x7 + 62x7) until the coming of "Messiah the Prince." Those will be "times of distress," but the "plaza"(street) and "moat" (wall) will be rebuilt. The word *messiah* means "anointed one," and throughout this prophecy, it can refer to either the postexilic leaders Joshua and Zerubbabel (Zechariah 4:14; 6:10-15) or to Jesus Christ. The prophecy may be understood as referring to both.

After 434 years, the "Messiah will be cut off, but not for himself." (NKJV) This description fits with the crucifixion of Jesus, who died on the cross, not for his own sins but for the sins of humanity. Soon after the death of Jesus, the Romans came and destroyed "the city and the sanctuary" (AD 70). The Romans caused "the sacrifice and the oblation (offerings) to cease," (NKJV) and they defiled the altar with an abomination of desolation. Verse 27 seems to apply in three ways:

(1) To Daniel's earlier prophecies about Antiochus IV Epiphanes;

(2) To the Roman desolation of the Temple in AD 70; and

(3) To the "beast" of Revelation 13.

From the time of Daniel until now, scholars have attempted to construct a calendar of events that would match this prophecy of seventy weeks. Several difficulties prevent a clear reconstruction of the

9 Lesson Nine

exact calendar of events. First, should the numbers be taken literally or symbolically? The number seven is used throughout and normally symbolizes perfection. Second, is the prediction based on the ancient year of 360 days or on the modern year of 365 days? Third, will the prediction be fulfilled only in one way or in more than one way? The dispensational view is that the 70th week is the seven years of Great Tribulation. Therefore, between the 69th and 70th weeks, there is a gap that includes the entire Church Age. (For a chart of four major interpretations, see J.B. Payne, *Encyclopedia of Biblical Prophecy*, pp. 384–85).

The purpose of an "inductive Bible study" is to learn as much as possible about the biblical text at hand, in this case, the Book of Daniel. Therefore, we attempt to keep our interpretations within the confines of Daniel itself, without spending too much time in the Book of Revelation, which did not exist in Daniel's day. Therefore, I have tried to focus on the essential truth of Daniel's vision, while allowing for various possible unfoldings of the events that he describes. Although we cannot be certain how the future will develop, we can be sure that God has dealt with sin through the sacrifice of Jesus Christ. Also, we can be sure that Jesus will return to establish His kingdom.

In this Devote step of our Bible study, you strengthen your relationship to God. It is not enough to read and study the Bible—we must devote ourselves to serving and worshiping the God of the Bible. It is time to allow the Holy Spirit to speak to you on a deeper level. Basically, you should ask, "God, in light of what You have taught me in Your Word, what do You want me to do?" As you enter into this Devote section, consider the following:

1. By now you have become very familiar with this chapter of Daniel. Therefore, you are ready to let the passage speak to your heart, if you have not already done so. In this step, you should write down the effect this passage has on you as a believer. How does it make you feel? What emotions are brought to the surface as you read the text? Do you feel gratitude, joy, hope, love, heaviness, conviction, guilt, liberty, awe, amazement, or courage?

DANIEL 9:1-27

2. What do you want to do in response to this text?

_____
_____
_____
_____
_____

3. How has this text affected you? Do you sense a transformation of your heart? Do you desire a certain kind of transformation?

_____
_____
_____
_____
_____

In order for you to devote, dedicate, and commit your entire self in obedience to God, you will need His grace. Let us pause for prayer, asking God to lead us into deeper devotion.

PAUSE *for* PRAYER

Lord God, I thank You for this time of study in Your Word. I pray that the words of Daniel will be written on my heart and echo in my mind for the rest of the day. Holy Spirit, I thank You for leading me into truth. Please bring these words to my remembrance when I need them, so I can walk the way Jesus walked. Jesus, I thank You for dying for me. Teach me to obey these words so that I honor Your sacrifice and walk in a way that people will want what I have found in You. Heavenly Father, teach me how You want me to apply Your Word in my life. Show me where I need to specifically change so that I look more like Jesus. I ask all this in the precious name of Jesus, our Lord. Amen.

9 Lesson Nine

⳨ Disciple

The ministry of the prophet is a high calling. The prophets stand boldly and proclaim to God's people the Word of God. Prophets encounter the powerful presence of God through the means of dreams and visions (Numbers 12:6). The Lord speaks to His prophets by the Holy Spirit and imparts to them the Word of the Lord (2 Samuel 7:4). In these last days, the Spirit has been poured out upon all flesh, and our sons and daughters are prophesying (Acts 2:16-18; 11:27; 13:1; 15:32; 21:8-10; Romans 12:6; Ephesians 4:11).

The greatest prophets, however, not only were blessed to receive visions and revelations, but also were given the heavy responsibility of intercession. I think of Abraham, whose intercession for Sodom and Gomorrah resulted in the salvation of Lot and his family (Genesis 18:17-33). Consider Moses, who interceded for Israel in the wilderness (Exodus 32:7-14). I'm reminded of Samuel who prayed all night for king Saul (1 Samuel 15:11; see also 12:23). Then, there was Jeremiah, who interceded with such fervency that he is called the weeping prophet (Jeremiah 9:1). In the New Testament, we read about the apostle Paul, who prayed without ceasing for his churches (2 Corinthians 11:23-28). Of course, the greatest of all intercessors is Jesus, who "lives to make intercession" for us (Hebrews 7:25; Romans 8:34). Those who would call themselves prophets, must be willing to accept the burden of intercession along with the blessing of divine revelations. The ministry of the Holy Spirit is the ministry of intercession (Romans 8:26-27), and when the Church meets for worship, we are instructed to engage in intercession (1 Timothy 2:1-5).

Daniel is no exception. We have learned that Daniel was given great wisdom. He was anointed to interpret the dreams and visions of King Nebuchadnezzar and King Belshazzar (chapters 2–6). He was also gifted with his own revelations by means of dreams and visions (chapters 7–12). Here in chapter 9, however, Daniel is engaged in an even more meaningful and significant ministry—the ministry of intercession.

This week I commit to:

1. Respond to the Word of God like Daniel—with humility and prayer.//
2. Confess my sins to God and to confess the sins of my church.
3. Intercede for the body of Christ, for unbelievers, for the sick, and for the weak believers.
4. Fast along with my prayers.
5. Wait upon the Lord and be receptive when the Holy Spirit speaks to me.

In conclusion, Daniel's experience points us to two vital activities. First, his prayer demonstrates the importance and eternal significance of intercession. If we hope to be effective in the kingdom of God, we must develop and promote the ministry of intercession. Our church must be a "house of prayer for all the peoples" (Isaiah 56:7). Second, Daniel's prayer shows the value of both individual and corporate confession. Like David, we must pray, "Search me, O God, and know my heart: try me, and know my thoughts: and see if there be any hurtful way in me, and lead me in the everlasting way" (Psalm 139:23-24). However, we must also follow the directions of Joel, who pleaded with his people: "Consecrate a fast, call a solemn assembly; gather the elders and all the inhabitants of the land into the house of the Lord your God, and cry out to the Lord" (Joel 1:14 NKJV). The church is more than a gathering of individuals—it is the body of Christ and the family of God. It is time to seek the Lord through corporate confession.

In order for us to fulfill our callings as individuals and as the Church, we must be intercessors. Yes, some people are more gifted as intercessors than other people, but we all are called to intercede. As we study Daniel's prayer, may the Lord teach us all how to pray more effectively, so that we may be "Faithful Witnesses Through Prayer and Fasting."

ENLIVEN ENCOUNTERING GOD Through HIS WORD

LESSON TEN

DANIEL
10:1–12:13

FAITHFUL WITNESS IN LIGHT OF THE END

Lesson Ten

Daniel 10:1–12:13   10

Lesson Ten

Daniel 10:1–12:13

Faithful Witness in Light of the End

🔑 Key Verse

Those who have insight will shine brightly like the brightness of the expanse of heaven, and those who lead the many to righteousness, like the stars forever and ever (Daniel 12:3).

Introduction

We are living in uncertain times, challenging times, and frustrating times—but there is nothing new about that. The prophet Habakkuk, who lived more than 2500 years ago, was appalled by the violence, evil, and unrighteousness that he witnessed in his day. God's answer to the prophet's cry was "the just shall live by his faith" (Habakkuk 2:4 KJV). The church congregation that is addressed in the book of Hebrews also faced trying circumstances. Having left Judaism to become Christians, they were being persecuted, and some even had their property confiscated by the authorities (Hebrews 10:34). God's solution for them was "the just shall live by faith" (Hebrews 10:38 KJV). For Habakkuk, for the Hebrews, and for us, the heart of the gospel (according to the apostle Paul) is that "the just shall live by faith" (Romans 1:17; Galatians 3:11 KJV).

Living by faith means that we know—as Daniel knew—that God is sovereign [in control]. It means that we lay up our treasures in heaven, because where our treasure is, there our hearts are also (Luke 12:34). To live by faith is to "know that if the earthly tent we live in is destroyed, we have a building from God, an eternal house in heaven, not built by human hands" (2 Corinthians 5:1 NIV). To live by faith is to live in hope of the resurrection. The truth of the resurrection was revealed to the prophet Daniel, and

10 Lesson Ten

he was assured that he would rise up to receive his inheritance "at the end of the age" (Daniel 12:13). We, too, have that assurance that "the dead shall be raised incorruptible, and we shall be changed" (1 Corinthians 15:52 KJV).

You have made significant progress on the *Path to Faithful Witness*, your journey through the Book of Daniel. You have now come to Daniel's fourth revelation, which is the final vision in the Book of Daniel, and it is quite lengthy. Daniel's fourth and final revelation spans chapters 10, 11, and 12. The vision takes place in the third year of Cyrus, king of Persia. It was 536 BC, three years after Cyrus had decreed that the Jews could return to Jerusalem (Ezra 1:1-2). Up to 50,000 Jews had made the journey back to Judea in hopes of restoring the nation of Israel and rebuilding the temple of God. It was a time of hope, but it was a time of conflict and disappointment as well.

Let us pause for prayer as we prepare to enter the study of Daniel's final and climactic vision.

Pause for Prayer

Read the Key Verse at the beginning of the lesson, and pray that God may give you "insight" into the meaning and the significance of Daniel 10–12.

> Heavenly Father, I praise You for Your Word. I give You honor and glory for all You have revealed to us. With Your voice You created all of heaven and earth. How awesome, perfect, and wonderful are all Your ways. Above all, You are seated on Your throne, to reign in steadfast love and mercy (Psalm 8). Let my heart and mind be thankful for this amazing gift. Every good gift, including Your Word, comes from You. I thank You for the wisdom You provide. I give You thanks for Your love and mercy toward me (Psalm 136). Lord, please open my eyes to the truth of Your Word. I pray for wisdom as I prepare to read Your Word, clarity for while I read, and discernment as I apply Your Word to my heart. Let Your Word change my character and my actions. I pray that the truth I find here will transform my heart and mind to follow more fully after You (James 1:5, 22-25). I pray that You will use Your Word to convict and correct me. Show me how I am falling short and how I must change. Search my heart. Cleanse me from my sin. Wash me clean with the truth of Your Word, and set me on the right path again. I pray all of these things in the name of Jesus. Amen.

DANIEL 10:1–12:13 | 10

THE TEXT

Daniel 10:1–12:13 NKJV

¹In the third year of Cyrus king of Persia a message was revealed to Daniel, whose name was called Belteshazzar. The message *was* true, but the appointed time *was* long; and he understood the message, and had understanding of the vision. ²In those days I, Daniel, was mourning three full weeks. ³I ate no pleasant food, no meat or wine came into my mouth, nor did I anoint myself at all, till three whole weeks were fulfilled.

⁴Now on the twenty-fourth day of the first month, as I was by the side of the great river, that *is,* the Tigris, ⁵I lifted my eyes and looked, and behold, a certain man clothed in linen, whose waist *was* girded with gold of Uphaz! ⁶His body *was* like beryl, his face like the appearance of lightning, his eyes like torches of fire, his arms and feet like burnished bronze in color, and the sound of his words like the voice of a multitude.

⁷And I, Daniel, alone saw the vision, for the men who were with me did not see the vision; but a great terror fell upon them, so that they fled to hide themselves. ⁸Therefore I was left alone when I saw this great vision, and no strength remained in me; for my vigor was turned to frailty in me, and I retained no strength. ⁹Yet I heard the sound of his words; and while I heard the sound of his words I was in a deep sleep on my face, with my face to the ground.

¹⁰ Suddenly, a hand touched me, which made me tremble on my knees and *on* the palms of my hands. ¹¹And he said to me, "O Daniel, man greatly beloved, understand the words that I speak to you,

10 Lesson Ten

and stand upright, for I have now been sent to you." While he was speaking this word to me, I stood trembling.

[12] Then he said to me, "Do not fear, Daniel, for from the first day that you set your heart to understand, and to humble yourself before your God, your words were heard; and I have come because of your words. [13] But the prince of the kingdom of Persia [*Evil spirit*] withstood me twenty-one days; and behold, Michael [*Angel*], one of the chief princes, came to help me, for I had been left alone there with the kings [*Earthly Kings*] of Persia. [14] Now I have come to make you understand what will happen to your people in the latter days, for the vision *refers* to *many* days yet *to come*."

[15] When he had spoken such words to me, I turned my face toward the ground and became speechless. [16] And suddenly, *one* having the likeness of the sons of men touched my lips; then I opened my mouth and spoke, saying to him who stood before me, "My lord, because of the vision my sorrows have overwhelmed me, and I have retained no strength. [17] For how can this servant of my lord talk with you, my lord? As for me, no strength remains in me now, nor is any breath left in me."

[18] Then again, *the one* having the likeness of a man touched me and strengthened me. [19] And he said, "O man greatly beloved, fear not! Peace *be* to you; be strong, yes, be strong!"

So when he spoke to me I was strengthened, and said, "Let my lord speak, for you have strengthened me."

[20] Then he said, "Do you know why I have come to you? And now I must return to fight with the prince of Persia; and when I have gone forth, indeed the prince of Greece will come. [21] But I will tell you what is noted in the Scripture of Truth. (No one upholds me against these, except Michael your prince.)

DANIEL 10:1–12:13 **10**

[Chapters 10–12 comprise one vision; but, because of its great length, we will not discuss chapter 11 in great detail. Instead, we will just point out key elements and provide a chart of historical events.]

11 (¹ "Also in the first year of Darius the Mede, I, *even* I, stood up to confirm and strengthen him.) ² And now I will tell you the truth: Behold, three more kings will arise in Persia, and the fourth shall be far richer than *them* all; by his strength, through his riches, he shall stir up all against the realm of Greece. ³ Then a mighty king shall arise, who shall rule with great dominion, and do according to his will. ⁴ And when he has arisen, his kingdom shall be broken up and divided toward the four winds of heaven, but not among his posterity nor according to his dominion with which he ruled; for his kingdom shall be uprooted, even for others besides these.

⁵ "Also the king of the South shall become strong, as well as *one* of his princes; and he shall gain power over him and have dominion. His dominion *shall be* a great dominion. ⁶ And at the end of *some* years they shall join forces, for the daughter of the king of the South shall go to the king of the North to make an agreement; but she shall not retain the power of her authority, and neither he nor his authority shall stand; but she shall be given up, with those who brought her, and with him who begot her, and with him who strengthened her in *those* times. ⁷ But from a branch of her roots *one* shall arise in his place, who shall come with an army, enter the fortress of the king of the North, and deal with them and prevail. ⁸ And he shall also carry their gods captive to Egypt, with their princes *and* their precious articles of silver and gold; and he shall continue *more* years than the king of the North.

⁹ "Also *the king of the North* shall come to the kingdom of the king of the South, but shall return to his own land. ¹⁰ However his sons shall stir up strife, and assemble a multitude of great forces; and *one* shall certainly come and overwhelm and pass through; then he shall return to his fortress and stir up strife.

10 Lesson Ten

¹¹ "And the king of the South shall be moved with rage, and go out and fight with him, with the king of the North, who shall muster a great multitude; but the multitude shall be given into the hand of his *enemy*. ¹² When he has taken away the multitude, his heart will be lifted up; and he will cast down tens of thousands, but he will not prevail. ¹³ For the king of the North will return and muster a multitude greater than the former, and shall certainly come at the end of some years with a great army and much equipment.

¹⁴ "Now in those times many shall rise up against the king of the South. Also, violent men of your people shall exalt themselves in fulfillment of the vision, but they shall fall. ¹⁵ So the king of the North shall come and build a siege mound, and take a fortified city; and the forces of the South shall not withstand *him*. Even his choice troops *shall have* no strength to resist. ¹⁶ But he who comes against him shall do according to his own will, and no one shall stand against him. He shall stand in the Glorious Land with destruction in his power.

¹⁷ "He shall also set his face to enter with the strength of his whole kingdom, and upright ones with him; thus shall he do. And he shall give him the daughter of women to destroy it; but she shall not stand *with him*, or be for him. ¹⁸ After this he shall turn his face to the coastlands, and shall take many. But a ruler shall bring the reproach against them to an end; and with the reproach removed, he shall turn back on him. ¹⁹ Then he shall turn his face toward the fortress of his own land; but he shall stumble and fall, and not be found.

²⁰ "There shall arise in his place one who imposes taxes *on* the glorious kingdom; but within a few days he shall be destroyed, but not in anger or in battle. ²¹ And in his place shall arise a vile person, to

whom they will not give the honor of royalty; but he shall come in peaceably, and seize the kingdom by intrigue. ²² With the force of a flood they shall be swept away from before him and be broken, and also the prince of the covenant. ²³ And after the league *is made* with him he shall act deceitfully, for he shall come up and become strong with a small *number of* people. ²⁴ He shall enter peaceably, even into the richest places of the province; and he shall do *what* his fathers have not done, nor his forefathers: he shall disperse among them the plunder, spoil, and riches; and he shall devise his plans against the strongholds, but *only* for a time.

²⁵ "He shall stir up his power and his courage against the king of the South with a great army. And the king of the South shall be stirred up to battle with a very great and mighty army; but he shall not stand, for they shall devise plans against him. ²⁶ Yes, those who eat of the portion of his delicacies shall destroy him; his army shall [1]be swept away, and many shall fall down slain. ²⁷ Both these kings' hearts *shall be* bent on evil, and they shall speak lies at the same table; but it shall not prosper, for the end *will* still *be* at the appointed time. ²⁸ While returning to his land with great riches, his heart shall be *moved* against the holy covenant; so he shall do *damage* and return to his own land.

²⁹ "At the appointed time he shall return and go toward the south; but it shall not be like the former or the latter. ³⁰ For ships from Cyprus shall come against him; therefore he shall be grieved, and return in rage against the holy covenant, and do *damage.*

"So he shall return and show regard for those who forsake the holy covenant. ³¹ And forces shall be mustered by him, and they shall defile the sanctuary fortress; then they shall take away the daily *sacrifices,* and place *there* the abomination of desolation. ³² Those who do wickedly against the covenant he shall corrupt with flattery; but the people who know their God shall be strong, and carry out *great exploits*. ³³ And those of the people who understand shall instruct many; yet *for many* days they shall fall by sword and flame, by captivity and plundering. ³⁴ Now when they fall, they shall be aided with a little help; but many shall join with them by intrigue. ³⁵ And *some* of those of understanding shall fall, to refine them, purify *them,* and make *them* white, *until* the time of the end; because *it is* still for the appointed time.

³⁶ "Then the king shall do according to his own will: he shall exalt and magnify himself above every god, shall speak blasphemies against the God of gods, and shall prosper till the wrath has been accomplished; for what has been determined shall be done. ³⁷ He shall regard neither the God of his fathers nor the desire of women, nor regard any god; for he shall exalt himself above *them* all. ³⁸ But in their place he shall honor a god of fortresses; and a god which his fathers did not know he shall honor with gold and silver, with precious stones and pleasant things. ³⁹ Thus he shall act against the strongest fortresses with a foreign god, which he shall acknowledge, *and* advance *its* glory; and he shall cause them to rule over many, and divide the land for gain.

⁴⁰ "At the time of the end the king of the South shall attack him; and the king of the North shall come against him like a whirlwind, with chariots, horsemen, and with many ships; and he shall enter the countries, overwhelm *them,* and pass through. ⁴¹ He shall also enter the Glorious Land, and many *countries* shall be overthrown; but these shall escape from his hand: Edom, Moab, and the prominent people of Ammon. ⁴² He shall stretch out his hand against the countries, and the land of Egypt shall not escape. ⁴³ He shall have power over the treasures of gold and silver, and over all the precious things of Egypt; also the Libyans and Ethiopians *shall follow* at his heels. ⁴⁴ But news from the east and the north

shall trouble him; therefore he shall go out with great fury to destroy and annihilate many. ⁴⁵ And he shall plant the tents of his palace between the seas and the glorious holy mountain; yet he shall come to his end, and no one will help him.

12 ¹"At that time Michael shall stand up, the great prince who stands *watch* over the sons of your people; and there shall be a time of trouble, such as never was since there was a nation, *even* to that time. And at that time your people shall be delivered, every one who is found written in the book. ² And many of those who sleep in the dust of the earth shall awake, some to everlasting life, some to shame *and* everlasting contempt. ³ Those who are wise shall shine like the brightness of the firmament, and those who turn many to righteousness like the stars forever and ever. ⁴ "But you, Daniel, shut up the words, and seal the book until the time of the end; many shall run to and fro, and knowledge shall increase."

⁵ Then I, Daniel, looked; and there stood two others, one on this riverbank and the other on that riverbank. ⁶ And *one* said to the man clothed in linen, who *was* above the waters of the river, "How long shall the fulfillment of these wonders *be*?"

⁷ Then I heard the man clothed in linen, who *was* above the waters of the river, when he held up his right hand and his left hand to heaven, and swore by Him who lives forever, that *it shall be* for a time, times, and half *a time;* and when the power of the holy people has been completely shattered, all these *things* shall be finished.

⁸ Although I heard, I did not understand. Then I said, "My lord, what *shall be* the end of these *things?*"

⁹ And he said, "Go *your way,* Daniel, for the words *are* closed up and sealed till the time of the end. ¹⁰ Many shall be purified, made white, and refined, but the wicked shall do wickedly; and none of the wicked

10 Lesson Ten

shall understand, but the wise shall understand. ¹¹ "And from the time *that* the daily *sacrifice* is taken away, and the abomination of desolation is set up, *there shall be* one thousand two hundred and ninety days. ¹² Blessed *is* he who waits, and comes to the one thousand three hundred and thirty-five days. ¹³ "But you, go *your way* till the end; for you shall rest, and will arise to your inheritance at the end of the days."

Discover

By this time, you have learned how to use the Discover step to dig into the text and learn the Who? What? When? Where? and Why? of Daniel's message. It is important that you ask these questions of the text so that you can uncover (that is, "Dis-cover") the important elements in the text.

The following Helping Questions will help you to discern the message of Daniel chapters 10–12.

Sample Helping Questions

1. Read through chapters 10–12 and attempt to outline the passage for yourself. Write your outline below. You may want to list the entirety of chapter 11 as "Historical Survey of Intertestamental Period." (Note: The number of lines may or may not match the number of sections in your outline.)

Daniel 10:1–12:13

2. Daniel's fourth revelation is described as "a message" that was "revealed" (10:1). In Hebrew, the "message" is *davar*, which is often translated "word." Thus, Daniel's description is a variation on the more familiar phrase, "The Word of the Lord came to …" a certain prophet (e.g., Genesis 15:1; 1 Samuel 15:10; Isaiah 38:4; Jeremiah 1:2; Ezekiel 1:3; Hosea 1:1). In Daniel's case, we read that a "message (of the Lord) was revealed to Daniel." When was this word revealed to Daniel?

Lesson Ten

3. We are reminded of Daniel's Babylonian name, which has not been mentioned since chapter 5. He was given the name Belteshazzar in Daniel 1:7, near the beginning of the book. By hearing the name again, here in the final vision, we are drawn to connect the end of the book with its beginning. We are reminded that Daniel is a captive, living in a foreign land, and subject to the power of a foreign monarch. How does Daniel describe the message that came to him in the vision?

_____
_____
_____
_____

4. Daniel explains that he was "mourning" for 21 days. It may be significant that even though Daniel mourned for 21 days, he does not use the Hebrew number 21. Instead, he states that he was mourning for "three sevens." The Book of Daniel uses the number "seven" as a symbol for perfection and completion; and seven days would be a normal time for complete mourning (e.g. 1 Samuel 31:13). Therefore, three sevens would suggests triple perfection. In the Old Testament, the people would practice the mourning rituals for a variety of reasons: death in the family, sickness, national crisis, repentance, or any other kind of sorrow (e.g. Exodus 33:4; 1 Samuel 6:19; Nehemiah 1:4; Ezra 10:6). We are not told why Daniel is in mourning; but in light of his confession and intercession in the previous chapter, perhaps he is mourning again over the disobedience of his people. What does verse 12 suggest as Daniel's reasons for mourning?

_____
_____
_____
_____

5. Describe Daniel's circumstances. Where was he (verse 4)? What did he see (verse 5)?

_____
_____

DANIEL 10:1–12:13   **10**

6. Describe the "person" that Daniel saw (verses 5-6).

7. How did Daniel respond physically to the vision (verses 7-10)?

8. According to verses 11 and 19, what was God's opinion of Daniel?

9. According to verses 12-13, when did God hear Daniel's prayer and dispatch the messenger to Daniel? What hindered the messenger from reaching Daniel? Who helped the messenger?

221

Lesson Ten

10. What is the purpose of the messenger's visit to Daniel (verse 14)?

11. How did Daniel respond in verses 15-18?

12. This messenger is fighting against someone; who is it (verse 20)?

Daniel 11:2-39 surveys the history of the intertestamental period from the Persian kingdom up to the Roman Empire. It will not be possible for us to comment on every detail of this history; therefore, we have provided a verse-by-verse account of the events.

DANIEL 10:1–12:13 | **10**

THE BIBLICAL TEXT	HISTORICAL EVENTS
²And now I will tell you the truth: Behold, three more kings will arise in Persia, and the fourth shall be far richer than *them* all; by his strength, through his riches, he shall stir up all against the realm of Greece.	Persia (536–326 BC). The three kings are Cambyses, Smerdis, and Darius I Hystaspis.
³Then a mighty king shall arise, who shall rule with great dominion, and do according to his will. ⁴And when he has arisen, his kingdom shall be broken up and divided toward the four winds of heaven, but not among his posterity nor according to his dominion with which he ruled; for his kingdom shall be uprooted, even for others besides these.	Greece under Alexander the Great (326–323 BC).
⁵"Also the king of the South shall become strong, as well as *one* of his princes; and he shall gain power over him and have dominion. His dominion *shall be* a great dominion.	Ptolemy I rules over Egypt (323–285 BC).
⁶And at the end of *some* years they shall join forces, for the daughter of the king of the South shall go to the king of the North to make an agreement; but she shall not retain the power of her authority, and neither he nor his authority shall stand; but she shall be given up, with those who brought her, and with him who begot her, and with him who strengthened her in *those* times.	Bernice, Daughter of Ptolemy I, marries Antiochus II
⁷But from a branch of her roots *one* shall arise in his place, who shall come with an army, enter the fortress of the king of the North, and deal with them and prevail. ⁸And he shall also carry their gods captive to Egypt, with their princes *and* their precious articles of silver and gold; and he shall continue *more* years than the king of the North. ⁹"Also *the king of the North* shall come to the kingdom of the king of the South, but shall return to his own land.	Ptolemy III rules over Egypt (246–221 BC).

223

10 Lesson Ten

¹⁰ However his sons shall stir up strife, and assemble a multitude of great forces; and *one* shall certainly come and overwhelm and pass through; then he shall return to his fortress and stir up strife.

Seleucus and Antiochus III, sons of Ptolemy III (226–187 BC).

¹¹ "And the king of the South shall be moved with rage, and go out and fight with him, with the king of the North, who shall muster a great multitude; but the multitude shall be given into the hand of his *enemy*. ¹² When he has taken away the multitude, his heart will be ⁽ᵈ⁾lifted up; and he will cast down tens of thousands, but he will not prevail.

Ptolemy IV rules Egypt (221–203 BC).

¹³ For the king of the North will return and muster a multitude greater than the former, and shall certainly come at the end of some years with a great army and much equipment. ¹⁴ "Now in those times many shall rise up against the king of the South. Also, violent men of your people shall exalt themselves in fulfillment of the vision, but they shall fall. ¹⁵ So the king of the North shall come and build a siege mound, and take a fortified city; and the forces of the South shall not withstand *him*. Even his choice troops *shall have* no strength to resist.

Ptolemy V rules Egypt (203–181 BC).

¹⁶ But he who comes against him shall do according to his own will, and no one shall stand against him. He shall stand in the Glorious Land with destruction in his power.

Antiochus III controls Israel by 197 BC.

¹⁷ "He shall also set his face to enter with the strength of his whole kingdom, and ⁽ᵈ⁾upright ones with him; thus shall he do. And he shall give him the daughter of women to destroy it; but she shall not stand *with him*, or be for him.

Antiochus gives Cleopatra to Ptolemy V (194 BC).

¹⁸ After this he shall turn his face to the coastlands, and shall take many. But a ruler shall bring the reproach against them to an end; and with the reproach removed, he shall turn back on him. ¹⁹ Then he shall turn his face toward the fortress of his own land; but he shall stumble and fall, and not be found.

Antiochus defeated by Romans (190 BC).

DANIEL 10:1–12:13 — 10

20 "There shall arise in his place one who imposes taxes *on* the glorious kingdom; but within a few days he shall be destroyed, but not in anger or in battle.

Seleucus IV oppresses Israel (187–175 BC).

21 And in his place shall arise a vile person, to whom they will not give the honor of royalty; but he shall come in peaceably, and seize the kingdom by intrigue. 22 With the [i]force of a flood they shall be swept away from before him and be broken, and also the prince of the covenant. 23 And after the league *is made* with him he shall act deceitfully, for he shall come up and become strong with a small *number of* people. 24 He shall enter peaceably, even into the richest places of the province; and he shall do *what* his fathers have not done, nor his forefathers: he shall disperse among them the plunder, spoil, and riches; and he shall devise his plans against the strongholds, but *only* for a time. 25 "He shall stir up his power and his courage against the king of the South with a great army. And the king of the South shall be stirred up to battle with a very great and mighty army; but he shall not stand, for they shall devise plans against him. 26 Yes, those who eat of the portion of his delicacies shall destroy him; his army shall [ii]be swept away, and many shall fall down slain. 27 Both these kings' hearts *shall be* bent on evil, and they shall speak lies at the same table; but it shall not prosper, for the end *will* still *be* at the appointed time.

Antiochus IV Epiphanes gains control of the Middle East (175–164 BC).

28 While returning to his land with great riches, his heart shall be *moved* against the holy covenant; so he shall do *damage* and return to his own land. 29 "At the appointed time he shall return and go toward the south; but it shall not be like the former or the latter. 30 For ships from Cyprus shall come against him; therefore he shall be grieved, and return in rage against the holy covenant, and do *damage*. "So he shall return and show regard for those who forsake the holy covenant.

Antiochus IV Epiphanes attacks Jerusalem.

10 Lesson Ten

³¹ And ⁽ᵒ⁾forces shall be mustered by him, and they shall defile the sanctuary fortress; then they shall take away the daily *sacrifices,* and place *there* the abomination of desolation. ³² Those who do wickedly against the covenant he shall ⁽ᵒ⁾corrupt with flattery; but the people who know their God shall be strong, and carry out *great exploits.* ³³ And those of the people who understand shall instruct many; yet *for many* days they shall fall by sword and flame, by captivity and plundering. ³⁴ Now when they fall, they shall be aided with a little help; but many shall join with them by ⁽ᵖ⁾intrigue. ³⁵ And *some* of those of understanding shall fall, to refine them, purify *them,* and make *them* white, *until* the time of the end; because *it is* still for the appointed time.

Antiochus IV Epiphanes desecrates the Temple (165 BC).
Antiochus persecutes the Jews.

³² Those who do wickedly against the covenant he shall corrupt with flattery; but the people who know their God shall be strong, and carry out *great exploits.*

Jews rebel against Antiochus (see 1 Maccabees 3–4).

³⁶ "Then the king shall do according to his own will: he shall exalt and magnify himself above every god, shall speak blasphemies against the God of gods, and shall prosper till the wrath has been accomplished; for what has been determined shall be done. ³⁷ He shall regard neither the God of his fathers nor the desire of women, nor regard any god; for he shall exalt himself above *them* all. ³⁸ But in their place he shall honor a god of fortresses; and a god which his fathers did not know he shall honor with gold and silver, with precious stones and pleasant things. ³⁹ Thus he shall act against the strongest fortresses with a foreign god, *which* he shall acknowledge, *and* advance *its* glory; and he shall cause them to rule over many, and divide the land for ⁽ʳ⁾gain.

Antiochus' actions described in more detail.

DANIEL 10:1–12:13   10

⁴⁰"At the time of the end the king of the South shall attack him; and the king of the North shall come against him like a whirlwind, with chariots, horsemen, and with many ships; and he shall enter the countries, overwhelm *them,* and pass through. ⁴¹He shall also enter the Glorious Land, and many *countries* shall be overthrown; but these shall escape from his hand: Edom, Moab, and the prominent people of Ammon. ⁴²He shall stretch out his hand against the countries, and the land of Egypt shall not escape. ⁴³He shall have power over the treasures of gold and silver, and over all the precious things of Egypt; also the Libyans and Ethiopians *shall follow* at his heels. ⁴⁴But news from the east and the north shall trouble him; therefore he shall go out with great fury to destroy and annihilate many.

⁴⁵And he shall plant the tents of his palace between the seas and the glorious holy mountain; yet he shall come to his end, and no one will help him.

Antiochus IV dies of disease.

13. As we pick up with chapter 12, the scene shifts entirely to the end of this age. Does Daniel 12:1 appear to be what we call the Great Tribulation (see Matthew 24:21)?

_____

_____

14. Michael the archangel will stand up to protect the Jewish people from those who wish to destroy them. During the time of tribulation, everyone whose name is "found written in the book" can be assured of deliverance. What "book" is Daniel talking about? (Compare Revelation 21:27; 13:8; and 20:15.)

_____

_____

_____

_____

_____

10 Lesson Ten

15. According to Daniel 12:2-3, what happens at the Resurrection? How are the righteous described?

16. What is Daniel told to do with the message that he has been given (12:4)?

17. Daniel now sees the figures of three people. Two are standing on either side of the river, and the other one, dressed in linen, is standing upon the water of the river. One of the two asked, "How long shall the fulfillment of these wonders be?" (12:6 NKJV), and the man clothed in linen replied, "it shall be for a time, times, and half a time," which means three and one-half years. But Daniel did not understand. He is probably thinking, *Three and one-half years from when?* That is, when does the time start? Therefore, Daniel asks again, "What shall be the end of these things?" But the man dressed in linen does not give the answer. Why is the answer withheld from Daniel? What is Daniel told to do (12:9, 13)?

DANIEL 10:1–12:13 — 10

18. Despite the sealing of the vision, Daniel is given the assurance that God is at work. What will the righteous do? What will the wicked do? Will the wicked understand?

The apostle Paul wrote that our vision is "dim," and we "know in part" (1 Corinthians 13:12). Nevertheless, we know enough—enough to hold fast to God's unchanging hand.

By working through these Helping Questions, you have already discovered how significant this vision is. One way that the Holy Spirit can reveal the great truths contained in this lesson is for you to prayerfully make up your own Helping Questions. As the Spirit guides you in creating your own questions, the deep meanings of the text will become clearer to you. Re-read the passage and take a moment to develop some of your own Helping Questions. Be sure to do your best to answer the questions you have created. This will help you to grapple more deeply with Daniel's message. In this way, you will extract even more facts from Daniel 10–12.

Your Helping Questions

10 LESSON TEN

Your Helping Questions Continued

DISCERN

The Discern step is designed to bring to light the emphases, symbols, and patterns of Scripture. Once again, review the symbols, highlighting, and marking systems you have used in the previous Discern steps. Some of them should become second nature by now—that is what you want. When inductive study becomes the natural way that you approach Scripture, you know that you are really making progress.

If you see any difficult words or concepts in the biblical text, use your Bible dictionary, Google, Wikipedia, or the other resources listed at the beginning of this book to look up their meanings.

The following questions, comments, and tips may serve as food for thought as you apply the Discern step to Daniel 10–12.

Daniel 10:1–12:13   10

1. How does the figure in the vision (verses 5-6) resemble John's description of the resurrected Jesus (Revelation 1:13-15)? Is it reasonable to assume that Jesus is the person who appeared to Daniel?

2. Compare Daniel 10:20-21 to Ephesians 6:12.

3. Before departing from Daniel, the heavenly messenger promises to show him that which is recorded in the "writing of truth" (10:21), which may refer to the Old Testament scriptures that had already been written. Or, it may be a symbolic heavenly book that reveals those things that God has determined to come to pass in the future. Heavenly books are mentioned, for example, in Daniel 7:10 and Revelation 20:12. What do you think the "writing of truth" signifies?

Lesson Ten

4. Once again, the messenger mentions the help that he receives from Michael, whom he calls "your prince." The word "your" is in the plural; therefore, it speaks of Daniel and all the Jews. Michael is evidently an archangel who is especially tasked with watching over the affairs of the Jewish people. The angel who is speaking had, in the past, given help to Michael. He says, "In the first year of Darius the Mede, I arose to be an encouragement and a protection for him" (11:1). How does this verse relate to spiritual warfare?

_____

_____

_____

_____

_____

_____

_____

_____

_____

_____

It is important that as we study, we remain in touch with the biblical text. We do not want our study method to disconnect us from the text itself. This is where the Pause for Prayer can really help. Step back from analyzing the text and pray that the Holy Spirit will open your eyes to the thought patterns found in the text. More than anything you have done thus far, the influence of the Holy Spirit will lead you into all truth (John 16:13).

Pause for Prayer

The psalmist affirms the value of the Word of God and the importance of obedience to God's commandments. As you prepare to pull everything together, pray for God's guidance and wisdom. At the end of your prayer, reflect on the following words from Psalm 119:

> "Your word is a lamp to my feet and a light to my path.
>
> I have sworn and confirmed that I will keep Your righteous judgments.
>
> I am afflicted very much; revive me, O LORD, according to Your word.

DANIEL 10:1–12:13   10

Accept, I pray, the freewill offerings of my mouth, O Lord, and teach me Your judgments.

My life is continually in my hand, yet I do not forget Your law.

The wicked have laid a snare for me, yet I have not strayed from Your precepts.

Your testimonies I have taken as a heritage forever, for they are the rejoicing of my heart.

I have inclined my heart to perform Your statutes forever, to the very end.

I hate the double-minded, but I love Your law.

You are my hiding place and my shield; I hope in Your word" (Psalm 119:105-114 NKJV).

In the wonderful name of Jesus, we pray. Amen.

→Pulling It All Together←

The Discover and Discern steps have given you a thorough knowledge of Daniel 10–12. Sometimes, when we study the Bible in detail, we can lose sight of the "big picture." So, go back and read Daniel 10–12 and study all your Helping Questions and their answers. You might want to take notes on all you have *discovered* thus far and list your discoveries in the Summarize Your Findings section below.

Summarize Your Findings

_____
_____
_____
_____
_____
_____
_____
_____

Lesson Ten

Summarize Your Findings Continued

The "Daniel Fast"

In order to underline the gravity of his request for understanding and the seriousness of his attempt to humble himself, Daniel restricted his diet and he did not anoint himself with fragrant oil (which symbolized joy). He ate no rich food, meat, or wine. By rich food, Daniel probably refers to the royal fare to which he was entitled as a member of the king's court. The date of his mourning would mean that he also avoided the rich foods that would have been part of the Feast of Unleavened Bread. The text does not reveal why Daniel did not fast from all food as he had done earlier (9:3). It should be noted that neither the word "fast" nor its synonym ("to afflict oneself") is found in Daniel 10; therefore, Daniel's practice should properly be described as abstinence rather than fasting. Daniel's experience suggests that if one is unable to practice normal fasting, abstinence from certain rich foods can be beneficial. It can add urgency to prayers and depth to spiritual passion. Abstinence can strengthen humility and help to direct prayer toward God. The New Testament example for the partial fast is John the Baptist, who ate "locusts and wild honey" (Matthew 3:4).

DANIEL 10:1–12:13 — 10

The "Little Horn" and the "Abomination of Desolation"

Daniel 11:21-45 expands on Daniel 8:9-10. The vision describes the rise of Antiochus IV Epiphanes, a "vile person" who opposes the "prince of the covenant," who is the high priest of God's Temple in Jerusalem. Antiochus killed Onias III, the Jewish high priest in 171 BC.

After a brief conflict with Egypt (vv. 25-27), Antiochus returns to Jerusalem and continues to oppose the "holy covenant" and the Jewish people. He forbids the worship of Jehovah, takes away the Jewish sacrifices, and requires everyone to worship Zeus. Antiochus pollutes the sanctuary by building an altar to Zeus and by offering a pig in the Jerusalem Temple. This act is called the abomination of desolation.

We discussed earlier that most interpreters believe one of two views of Daniel's visions. Either they were fulfilled in history, or they are yet to be fulfilled in the last days leading up to the second advent of Jesus. I would suggest that both are true. Some elements of Daniel's prophecies were literally fulfilled during the intertestamental period. The Persian Empire arose and fell, and so did the Greek Empire. An evil general named Antiochus IV Epiphanes attacked the Jews and defiled the Temple in Jerusalem, but God gave the Jews victory and restored the Temple to its rightful place. However, these fulfilments only partially complete the picture that is painted in Daniel's dreams and visions. These visions are symbolic, prophetic, and represent a repetition of evil throughout history. The abomination of desolation was first committed by Antiochus, but Jesus talked about it as something yet to happen in the future. He said, "Therefore when you see the 'abomination of desolation,' spoken of by Daniel the prophet, standing in the holy place ... then there will be great tribulation, such as has not been since the beginning of the world until this time, no, nor ever shall be. And unless those days were shortened, no flesh would be saved; but for the elect's sake those days will be shortened" (Matthew 24:14-22 NKJV). The abomination of desolation was repeated in AD 70 by the Romans, when they invaded Jerusalem. The actions of Antiochus and of the Romans, however, are prophetic of the last days, when the same desecration will be committed before the return of Jesus. Old

Daniel before King Cyrus
by Rembrandt

Testament prophecies often combine both short-term and long-term predictions in a way that we find difficult to separate.

In these last days—as it was in the time of Antiochus and as it was in the time of the Romans—"the people who know their God shall be strong, and carry out great exploits" (11:32 NKJV). During times of testing, the people of God must be prepared to "understand" and to "instruct" (11:33 NKJV), even though they may face death by "sword, by flame, by captivity, and by plundering." These perilous times are for testing, "and to purify, and make them white, until the time of the end" (11:35 NKJV).

Devote

In this step of our Bible study, you strengthen your relationship to God. It is not enough to read and study the Bible—we must devote ourselves to serving and worshiping the God of the Bible. It is time to allow the Holy Spirit to speak to you on a deeper level. Basically, you should ask, "God, in light of what You have taught me in Your Word, what do You want me to do?" As you enter into this Devote section, consider the following:

1. By now you have become very familiar with this chapter of Daniel. Therefore, you are ready to let the passage speak to your heart, if you have not already done so. In this step, you should write down the effect this passage has on you as a believer. How does it make you feel? What emotions are brought to the surface as you read the text? Do you feel gratitude, joy, hope, love, heaviness, conviction, guilt, liberty, awe, amazement, or courage?

DANIEL 10:1–12:13   10

2. What do you want to do in response to this text? How does your response to Daniel's vision compare to his very visceral and physical response?

3. How has this text affected you? Do you sense a transformation of your heart? Do you desire a certain kind of transformation? Does Daniel 12 give you a longing for the return of Jesus?

10 Lesson Ten

Looking back on the Devote step and looking forward to the Disciple step, let us seek the Lord's favor. We want to be devoted disciples. Reflect on the message of Daniel 10–12 and pause for prayer that God will help you to devote yourself to its teachings.

Pause for Prayer

Father, Son, and Holy Spirit, holy is Your Word and perfect are Your ways. Let me be blessed by Your Word today as I mediate on Your precepts. Your promises are true. Your Word is faithful. Let me walk in the path of Your Word today. I pray that the words of my mouth come from *Your* truth. Let my thoughts be governed by *Your* commandments. I pray that You will bless this day as I seek to dwell in Your Word. (Father, I thank You that You have revealed Your love to us today. I invite You to send me out from here in the power of the Holy Spirit. Fan into flame the gifts that You have given to me. Come and reveal Your grace and truth to me today. For Yours is the kingdom, the power, and the glory, for ever and ever. Lord, Your Word is a lamp to my feet and a light to my path. Thank You that I can live in Your light and walk in Your truth. May the things that You have revealed to me continue to dwell in my heart and stir me to action. In the wonderful name of Jesus, we pray. Amen.

Disciple

There are six major themes that are woven through Daniel chapters 7–12:

(1) The height of human pride, especially represented in military power;

(2) An announcement of future deliverance;

(3) The importance of repentance;

(4) The spiritual powers that lie behind earthly kingdoms;

(5) The certainty of judgment for all who oppose the will of God; and

(6) The certainty of God's rule, which includes eternal blessings for God's people. Despite all present indicators to the contrary, God will be victorious in the end.

Daniel's final vision challenges us to be steadfast, even in perilous times. Daniel wants us to make up our minds whose side we are on, and stick with it. He emphasizes the responsibility of teaching, and

CONCLUDING REMARKS 11

of discipleship. The Book of Daniel encourages us to be faithful like Daniel, to pray like Daniel, to trust God like Daniel, and to have hope like Daniel.

This week I commit to:

1. Seek the Lord in prayer and fasting.

2. Be patient, knowing that God has already heard my prayers.

3. Trust in God's power and His wisdom as the Lord of history.

4. Be encouraged as God purifies and refines me (12:10).

5. Serve the Lord faithfully, while I watch for His return.

6. To be a "Faithful Witness in Light of the End" (12:13).

Remember that the Great Commission challenges us to "make disciples." That is, we must not only be concerned about our own spiritual well-being; but, we also must look after the spiritual needs of others. Look around you and be open to helping, guiding, and mentoring other believers who may benefit from your experience as a Christian. You should also be ready to share the good news of Jesus with unbelievers who cross your path. In so doing, you will be a *faithful witness*.

Lesson Ten

The inductive Bible study method has encouraged you to enter into various aspects of study. You have gathered data, posed questions to the text, highlighted important words and phrases, and summarized everything you have learned about Daniel 10–12. Now is the time to prayerfully seek the guidance of the Holy Spirit as you seek out the full meaning of this passage. You may want to jot down some notes as you meditate on your findings thus far. When you feel satisfied that you have a good grasp on all the features of this passage of Scripture, write out your interpretation. Do not worry that your interpretation may be different from someone else's interpretation. There is more than one way of describing the teachings of this biblical text, and just the activity of putting your thoughts into words will help you to remember the message of Daniel.

Your Interpretation

In this step, you will record your interpretations of this chapter of Daniel in the areas of Christian beliefs, practices, and spirituality. How does this biblical text inform our beliefs regarding the nature and character of God, the plans and purposes of God, the doctrines of salvation, sanctification, the baptism of the Holy Spirit, sin, healing, the last days, the family, the Church, etc.? Are there issues in this text that you do not understand or that cause you to be uncomfortable? Explain how this text may impact spiritual topics like prayer, fasting, witnessing, testimony, giving, study, worship, sacraments, etc. Write down any interpretations that relate to our beliefs, practices, or spirituality. In Daniel 10–12, we noted especially the new subject of spiritual warfare. What does this passage teach us about spiritual warfare? Daniel 12:2-3 brings to light the important topic of the Resurrection. What does Daniel reveal about the Resurrection (see also 12:13). Discuss other important topics as well.

Concluding Remarks   11

Concluding Remarks

In these ten Bible study lessons, we have read the Book of Daniel, and we have learned how to trust God in the midst of challenging times. In chapters 1–6, we heard the powerful stories about Daniel and his Hebrew friends, in which the kings of Babylon threatened to bring the faithful Jews to an end. In each case, however, God overruled the human rulers with amazing interventions that protected the Hebrews. In chapters 7–12, we studied mysterious visions of the end that unveiled the deeper dimensions of God's present and future sovereign rule. The visions have shown us that just as God ruled over the life and times of Daniel, God continues to rule over every earthly kingdom. Ultimately, God will bring all human kingdoms to an end, and He will establish His eternal kingdom with Jesus the Messiah as king.

The visions of Daniel are similar to the visions of John in the Book of Revelation, and the two books have a similar purpose. Visions of the end give us a broad picture of the future, but they are not designed to be a detailed calendar of events. I would like to say that this study has answered all your questions about the Book of Daniel; but, unfortunately, that is not the case. Dedicated and intelligent Bible scholars have wrestled with Daniel's prophecies for over 2000 years, and they have not reached agreement on the meaning of all the details. As I studied prominent prophecy teachers such as Clarence Larkin, C.I. Scofield, Finis Dake, and Tim LaHaye, I was surprised to learn that their interpretations of Daniel do not always agree. The purpose of an "inductive Bible study" is to learn as much as possible about the biblical text at hand—in this case, the Book of Daniel. Therefore, we have attempted to keep our interpretations as close as possible to the words of Daniel himself, without spending too much time in Matthew 24 or in the Book of Revelation, which did not exist in Daniel's day.

Although Daniel's prophecies still retain some mystery, his visions assure us that God is in control and that we can trust in Him. The visions of the end give us vibrant hope so that we can fulfill our mission as *faithful witnesses* of Jesus Christ until He returns. Even in the face of difficult challenges and persecution, we can live faithfully in the light of the end, as we look for the "blessed hope and glorious appearing of our great God and Savior Jesus Christ" (Titus 2:13 NKJV).

11   Concluding Remarks

Our Father who art in heaven,
Hallowed be Thy name.
Thy kingdom come. Thy will be done,
On earth as it is in heaven.
Give us this day our daily bread.
And forgive us our debts,
as we also have forgiven our debtors.
And do not lead us into temptation,
but deliver us from evil.
For Thine is the kingdom,
and the power,
and the glory,
forever.
Amen
(Matthew 6:9–13 NASB 1977)

About the Author

Lee Roy Martin is professor of Old Testament and Biblical Languages at the Pentecostal Theological Seminary in Cleveland, Tennessee. He received the B.A. in Biblical Education from Lee College (1977), the M.Div. from the Church of God Theological Seminary (1983), and the D.Th. in Old Testament from the University of South Africa (2007).

Professor Martin ministered as a pastor in the Church of God from 1977–2004. Ordained in 1983, he served as a district overseer, state Youth and CE Board member, state Council member, state Director of Ministerial Development, and state Ordination Board member. He has preached in Church of God State Conventions, Prayer Conferences, Youth Camps, and Pastors Conferences. He has taught at the Seminary since 1992, and he has taught courses at Lee University, Han Young University (Seoul), the Asian Seminary for Christian Ministry (Manila), the *Seminario Sudamericano* (Quito), *Seminaire Theologique de l'Eglise de Dieu en Haiti*, the Puerto Rico extension of the Pentecostal Theological Seminary (San Juan), and the North Central Spanish Academy (Chicago).

Martin has published several books, including *Living What We Believe: A Saved People* (Cleveland, TN: Church of God Adult Discipleship, 2018); *Biblical Hermeneutics: Essential Keys for Interpreting the Bible; Introduction to Biblical Hebrew*; and *The Unheard Voice of God: A Pentecostal Hearing of the Book of Judges*. Along with his 23 encyclopedia articles, book chapters, and book reviews, Dr. Martin has published 19 journal articles, including, "Longing for God: Psalm 63 and Pentecostal Spirituality;" "Delighting in the Torah: The Affective Dimension of Psalm 1;" "'Where Are All His Wonders?': The Exodus Motif in the Book of Judges;" and "Power to Save!?: The Role of the Spirit of the Lord in the Book of Judges."

In addition to his ministry of teaching, he serves as editor of the *Journal of Pentecostal Theology* (2008–present) and is a past president of the Society for Pentecostal Studies.

He married Karen Arlene Luke in 1975, and they have three children: Stephen (b. 1979), Michael (b. 1984), and Kendra (b. 1995). Stephen and his wife Marilyn have two boys, Joshua and Caleb. Karen and Lee Roy are deeply involved in their local church, Grace Community Church (Pastor Kevin Mendel), where Lee Roy serves as associate pastor.

This QR Code links to Dr. Martin's website: